Garland Studies
in Medieval Literature

Editors

Christopher Kleinhenz,
University of Wisconsin-Madison

Paul E. Szarmach,
State University of New York at Binghamton

Garland Studies
in Medieval Literature

PIERS PLOWMAN AND PROPHECY
An Approach to the C-Text

Theodore L. Steinberg

Volume 5
GARLAND STUDIES IN MEDIEVAL LITERATURE

Garland Publishing, Inc.
New York & London
1991

Library of Congress Cataloging-in-Publication Data

Steinberg, Theodore L., 1947–
    Piers Plowman and prophecy : an approach to the C-text / Theodore L.
Steinberg.
        p.   cm. — (Garland studies in medieval literature : v. 5)
(Garland reference library of the humanities : vol. 1367)
    Includes index.
    ISBN 0–8240–7074–7 (alk. paper)
    1. Langland, William, 1330?–1400? Piers the Plowman.
2. Prophecies in literature. I. Title. II. Series. III. Series:
Garland reference library of the humanities : vol. 1367.
PR2017.P74S74   1991
822'.1—dc20
                                                              90–49437
                                                              CIP

Printed on acid-free, 250-year-life paper
Manufactured in the United States of America

For
Gillian
Daniel
Miriam
and most of all
Phyllis

Contents

Preface of the General Editors

Garland Studies in Medieval Literature (GSML) is a series of interpretative and analytic studies of the Western European literatures of the Middle Ages. It includes both outstanding recent dissertations and book-length studies, giving junior scholars and their senior colleagues the opportunity to publish their research.

The editors welcome submissions representing any of the various schools of criticism and interpretation. Western medieval literature, with its broad historical span, multiplicity and complexity of language and literary traditions, and special problems of textual transmission and preservation as well as varying historical contexts, is both forbidding and inviting to scholars. It continues to offer rich materials for virtually every kind of literary approach that maintains a historical dimension. In establishing a series in an eclectic literature, the editors acknowledge and respect the variety of texts and textual possibilities and the "resisting reality" that confronts medievalists in several forms: on parchment, in mortar, or through icon. It is no mere imitative fallacy to be eclectic, empirical, and pragmatic in the face of this varied literary tradition that has so far defied easy formulation. The cultural landscape of the twentieth century is littered with the debris of broken monomyths predicated on the Middle Ages, for the autocratic Church and the Dark Ages or, conversely, the romanticized versions of love and chivalry.

The openness of the series means in turn that scholars, and particularly beginning scholars, need not pass an *a priori* test of "correctness" in their ideology, method, or critical position. The studies published in GSML must be true to their premises, complete within their articulated limits, and accessible to a multiple readership. Each study will advance the knowledge of the literature under discussion, opening it up for further consideration and creating intellectual value. It is also hoped that each volume, while bridging the gap between contemporary perspective and past reality, will make old texts new again. In this way the literature will remain primary, the method secondary.

In this fifth volume in the series, Theodore L. Steinberg studies what might be called the "mindscape" of *Piers Plowman*. Once considered "a windy poem" and a deadening text best consigned to the dustbin of history, William Langland's visionary pursuit of self and Christian society has emerged since mid-century as one of the masterpieces of Chaucer's time. Scholars and critics have begun not only to understand the intricacies of its many versions but also to appreciate and understand its poetics, the ground of its social and moral criticism, and above all its *curiosa felicitas*. Most might still agree that Langland is more medieval than Chaucer, but now more hear and perceive the strengths of this great work. The outpouring of books, articles, and papers are sure witnesses to the poem's appeal, as is the establishment of *The Yearbook of Langland Studies,* the new journal devoted to *Piers*, other similar alliterative verse, and the cultural background thereto. Steinberg contributes to this growing body of scholarship on *Piers* by suggesting one source of its power. Here "source" does not mean verifiable or documentary or evidentiary antecedent but rather imaginative wellspring. Steinberg argues that *Piers*, particularly in the C-text, is a poem inspired by the writings of the biblical prophets. He outlines the fourteenth-century background, discussing the idea of prophecy and how the biblical prophets were read as well as the role of such literary models as Wyclif and Joachim of Fiore. By an examination of specific aspects of the poem, Steinberg shows the imaginative connections between *Piers* and the prophets. Langland is, according to Steinberg, ". . . simply describing how, in biblical terms, this world can be made a better place in both an individual and a communal sense, as it was in the early days of the Church. . . ." What makes Steinberg's analysis so effective is his view that an understanding of Langland's prophetic stance is complementary to other approaches to the poem. The overall formulation here presented transcends the mire of close detail, an overattention to which can make *Piers* appear to be a string of local successes and a failure on the grand scale, and yet gives the poem a grounded coherence.

Those who wish more information about submitting their manuscripts to GSML may write to either of the series editors, but in general submissions in English and Germanic literatures should be addressed to Paul E. Szarmach and those in Romance literatures to Christopher Kleinhenz.

<table>
<tr><td>Christopher Kleinhenz</td><td>Paul E. Szarmach</td></tr>
<tr><td>University of Wisconsin-Madison</td><td>SUNY–Binghamton</td></tr>
</table>

FOREWORD

This work was begun after a series of conversations, extending over several years, at meetings of the International Congress on Medieval Studies at Western Michigan University. It represents an experiment, as all books represent an experiment. This particular experiment attempts to examine one particular sort of biblical influence on one of the most remarkable works of the Middle Ages. I have several hopes for this book. One is that it will increase our knowledge and understanding of *Piers Plowman*. Another is that it will expand our understanding of how the Bible was employed as a literary source during the Middle Ages. And another is that it will help us to see the continuing relevance for our own time of even so quintessentially medieval a work as *Piers Plowman*. I find these all to be fascinating subjects of study, and I also hope, therefore, that I have been able to convey that fascination in a profitable way, or as Langland would say, for the "comune profyt."

Whenever I begin to read a new book, I look at the preface and read the author's thanks to all who helped in the preparation of the book. I am reminded that the academic community is a community and that there is very little that we can accomplish in that community without the help of our colleagues. I am profoundly aware of the debt that I owe to others who have helped me with this book, and I am pleased to thank Minda Rae Amiran, Karen Mills-Courts, Jane Chance, and John Alford, who read various drafts or sections of the manuscript and made helpful comments, often more helpful than they may have suspected. I owe a special debt to M. Teresa Tavormina for her very close reading of the whole manuscript and for her numerous suggestions, which, I confess, were occasionally more thorough than I wanted to hear but which were always sound and thoughtful and which helped to make this a better book. I owe much, too, to Paul Szarmach, the editor of this series for Garland, and to the whole Garland staff. I am also indebted to Lillian Russell of the Walters Art Gallery in Baltimore, to the staff of Reed Library at the State University of New York at Fredonia, to Joanne Foeller for her extraordinary care in preparing the manuscript, and to the administration of the college for doing what they can to support both research and teaching despite yearly announcements of disappointing budget news.

My greatest debt, as always, is to my wife Phyllis and my children Gillian, Daniel, and Miriam, to whom this book is dedicated.

PREFACE

The steady accumulation of books, articles, and conference papers on various aspects of *Piers Plowman* testifies to the continuing power of that difficult and occasionally obscure poem. What is it about *Piers Plowman* that draws us to it? Sixteenth-century readers thought that the poem foretold the Reformation and therefore spoke directly to them. If they were somewhat simplistic about the first assumption, they were entirely accurate about the second. For literature from the past to be anything more than a historical curiosity, it must speak directly to a succession of audiences, and this is what *Piers Plowman* has done for much of the previous six centuries. It may not speak to a huge audience now, but the considerable attention it receives in contemporary criticism indicates, I hope, that the poem offers more than just an intellectual puzzle. This study of the poem is an attempt to understand one way in which the poem works, one source of its power.

The major point of this study is that *Piers Plowman*, especially in its third version, the C-Text, is a poem inspired by the writings of the biblical prophets. After a brief introductory chapter in which the problems to be discussed are presented, the book moves on to an examination of the biblical prophets, their backgrounds, their thoughts, and their literary techniques, as well as a consideration of the meaning of prophecy and the ways the prophets were read in the Middle Ages. The next chapter explores some of the factors in fourteenth-century England that may have prompted Langland to rely on the prophetic writings as literary models, including such matters as the influence of Wyclif and Joachim of Fiore and the popularity of dream visions.

The fourth chapter of the book establishes the relationship between *Piers Plowman* and the prophets by examining specific aspects of the poem and their prophetic sources in such areas as the call to prophecy and the structure of the poem. Finally, the book concludes by considering the implications of this relationship for our understanding of the poem, especially of such problematical matters as the poem's conclusion, the relationship between the individual and society, and the meaning of Dowel, Dobet, and Dobest.

The importance of this study goes beyond clarifying this difficult poem, for if my approach is correct, it means that it was possible for medieval readers to approach the Bible on a sophisticated literal level and to be aware of its literary qualities. It also means that we might profitably look for such awareness in other medieval works.

This point requires clarification from the outset. Speaking about the literal level as it was understood in the Middle Ages is not as simple as it might seem. Beryl Smalley illustrated the problem in her discussion of Hugh of Saint-Cher and Guerric of Saint-Quentin, both of whom commented on the works of Andrew of Saint Victor. For example, "Hugh, following Andrew, interpreted the text *Emitte agnum, Domine, dominatorem terrae* . . . (Is. xvi,1) as referring, not to the Advent of Christ, but to the giving of tribute by the Moabites. . . . Guerric first gives the interpretation of *agnum* as *Christum*, as the literal sense; then he sets out the view of 'the Jews and Andrew', only to reject it with a violence probably provoked by Hugh's acceptance of it. . . ." (Smalley 1946, 392). When I speak of the literal level, I mean the literal level as Andrew and Hugh conceived of it, that is as historical literalism, with close attention paid to what the words mean in themselves rather than to tropological or anagogical meanings. As Robert Crowley wrote in his prologue to *Piers Plowman* in 1571, in a view that often echoes my own, "Loke not upon this boke therfore, to talke of wonders paste or to come, but to amende thyne owne misse, which thou shalt fynd here most charitably rebuked."

As far as other medieval works are concerned, I hope that what I have to say here may also spur investigation into the ways in which other works use the Bible as a literary prototype. Several such studies already exist, such as David Jeffrey's study of the *House of Fame* and Ezekiel or Mary Clemente Davlin's examination of *Piers Plowman* and biblical wisdom literature, but the approach I am suggesting might profitably be applied, for instance, to the *Pearl*-poet or to other works of the Alliterative Revival.

I must emphasize that I offer this work not as an argument against other readings of the poem, and certainly not as the only way to view the poem, but as one more way to view it, an additional perspective that can add to our understanding of what Langland accomplished. John Alford has recently published *Piers Plowman: A Glossary of Legal Diction*, a work that studies the important legal aspects of the poem without claiming that they provide the only way to look at the poem. In fact, that book offers a view that complements this study. As with all great works of literature, what we see in Piers Plowman depends on where we stand to look at it, and the more observation points that we employ, the greater will our understanding be. This study, then, is not meant to exclude others but to complement them. I am examining one source of Langland's inspiration, what I consider one major source of the poem, but clearly there are many others. If I do not dwell on the others, it is because other students of the poem have done so. My subject is the role of the prophetic books in *Piers Plowman*, and that is what I shall consider, but I do not present that as a single-source argument. I am offering, as my subtitle indicates, an approach to the poem. I delight in acknowledging that there are other approaches as well. As Davlin says about her study, "This is neither a source study nor an argument for a new generic classification of *Piers Plowman*, but a brief proposal that a familiar group of texts served Langland as what Michael Riffaterre calls an 'intertext . . . a corpus of other texts . . . that shares its lexicon and its structures with the one we are reading'" (23).

ACKNOWLEDGMENTS

To AMS Press, Inc. for allowing me to quote from their edition of the Wyclif Bible.

To the University of California Press for allowing me to quote from Derek Pearsall's edition of the C-Text of *Piers Plowman*.

To *Bucknell Review* for allowing me to quote from my article "Isaiah the Poet," which originally appeared in Vol. 33:2 of that journal.

To *Christian Jewish Relations* for allowing me to quote from my article "The Jewish Presence in Middle English Literature," which originally appeared in Vol. 20:4 of that journal.

I. Introduction

"As a great medievalist recently complained: 'We know so little about these people. As we stir these cold ashes, a tongue of flame seems to dart out and flicker and die. We cannot feel sure of very much'" (McFarlane 9). The more we get to know about "these people," the better acquainted with them we become, the more caution we must adopt. It is so tempting for us to recreate them in our image, making them so like ourselves that they disappear; or it is tempting for us to recreate them in an image so different from our own that their concerns may seem irrelevant to anything we consider important. Somehow we must strike a balance, we must use the differences that separate us from our ancestors while at the same time we understand the profound links that tie us together. Surely this kind of problem is constantly faced by historians and anthropologists, who may discipline themselves with at least a pretense of scientific objectivity. Literary scholars, however, dealing as they do with the world of imaginative literature, confront an acute form of the dilemma. The ancient epic of *Gilgamesh*, which raises questions about human mortality, friendship, and purpose, seems so close to questions that we are still asking that we may feel ourselves to be directly in touch with the poet's mind, a feeling that is simultaneously real and illusory. As we read any work, we may feel that the writer is speaking directly to us, that the writer's concerns are our own, and, frequently, that the writer has adopted our attitudes toward those concerns. To the extent that literature transcends the passage of time, such feelings may be legitimate. And yet they are also dangerous, for they can lead to a homogenized view, a view that sees sameness everywhere. If we could only know what the author intended — and yet we know how problematical intentionality can be. Even when the author tells us, we may be misled. To understand Keats's poetry, how many of his letters should we read? To grasp *The Faerie Queene*, how seriously should we take Spenser's letter to Ralegh? Does Dante's letter to Can Grande really tell us how to read the *Comedy*? Whatever help — or hindrance — such authorial guidance may provide, we must always return to the literary work itself, recognizing — and perhaps trying to minimize — whatever personal prejudices we may bring with us.

1

Because, thankfully, literary study is not "scientific," we do not have to pretend to eliminate our prejudices. In fact we must not, for literature is to a large extent built on feelings. As we read *Piers Plowman*, we get the feeling that this poem is, somehow, an extraordinary work. What makes it so? Langland wrote no letters to explain what he thought he was doing, although the existence of three texts of his poem illustrates to some extent the evolution of what he thought he was doing. Thus, the argument of this study concerns what seems to have been the poet's intentions. Langland, who saw the world in terms of the Bible as the Bible was understood in late fourteenth-century England, wrote a work in which he undertook to play the role of a prophet.

A corollary to this argument is that *Piers Plowman* is an important work not only for literary history or for the development of medieval thought but for us, now. We must in no way slight the medieval provenance of the poem, but we must not make it so esoterically medieval that it becomes a mere curiosity. Chaucer, whose work is inherently more accessible and whose influence helped to shape the tradition and the language to which we are accustomed, does not seem as strange as Langland; and once we master his language and grasp certain fourteenth-century modes of thought, we may well feel comfortable with Chaucer. We cannot feel nearly so comfortable with Langland, just as we cannot feel comfortable with Isaiah or Jeremiah, for those prophets continue to remind us of how far we remain from any fulfillment of the divine ideals that they preached. Langland, seeing himself in their tradition, provides us with a similar reminder, even if we do not accept his medieval views or even his Christianity.

Piers Plowman, then, is in every way a startling poem, a work that was valued by its first readers and that, despite its apparent appeal today largely to students of medieval literature, has valuable things to say to modern readers. This point is worth exploring. As we read Chaucer, we may be — or should be — tempted to recognize his characters among our acquaintances. In our own microcosmic pilgrimages, surely we have met the Wife of Bath or the Miller or even the Knight. In fact one of the dangers in reading Chaucer is that he too easily becomes our contemporary. With Langland, the situation is almost the opposite. Langland often seems totally different from us, someone whose works we study to learn about the fourteenth century but whose language, methodology, and thought are separated from us by a tremendous gulf. We may number the Wife of Bath among our friends, but we surely do not know anyone like Langland's allegorical Resoun or even like the more nearly human characters such as Actyf, Piers himself, or the seemingly narcoleptic narrator Will, any of whom we would probably try to avoid. And if Chaucer is writing allegory, at least he encloses the kernel in an attractive shell: he tells good stories. Langland, quite simply, does not, nor, largely, does he intend to. At best he tells fragments of good stories and then moves on, abruptly, to something else, because he is not, after all, attempting to write the kind of mimetic realism that Chaucer used. Thus part of Langland's "foreignness" results from our attraction to realistic narratives and our puzzlement over just what kind of work Langland wrote. Moreover, as Donald Howard points out, once Chaucer had devised the structure for the *Canterbury Tales*, "he could think about and laugh at the very fabric of a society that seemed to be falling in pieces" (401). Chaucer and Langland saw the same society, but while Chaucer could laugh, Langland railed. We see in them very different reactions — perhaps we could loosely call them Horatian and Juvenalian — to the same situation.

These elements, among others, have distanced us from Langland and have led to a startling number of critical approaches to his work. At one extreme is Owst's description of Langland as "the comparatively simple English poet" (58), a judgment that is belied by most criticism of the poem but that is probably closer to the truth than may at first appear. Generally, however, critics have treated the poem as a complex work and have focused on its use of patristic exegesis, spiritual autobiography, the liturgy, medieval romance, or classical models to illustrate that complexity.

Despite such efforts — and despite their high quality — the poem continues to bewilder readers in a number of ways. Whatever one critic argues, another denies. For example, in talking about the plot of *Piers Plowman*, Mary Carruthers says, "*Piers* has 'no plot' not because nothing happens but because nothing that does happen seems very much to affect anything else that happens" (Carruthers 1982, 175), while Ruth Ames points out that "Even second-rate authors saw past, present, and future, heaven, earth, and hell all related and interrelated under God, both in time and in eternity" (8), implying that everything that happens in *Piers*, like everything that happens in the world, affects everything else. Comparable disagreements can be found on such important questions as Langland's learning (he was intimately familiar with the writings of the Church Fathers — or he was not) and his relationship to Wyclif (he was a follower of Wyclif — or Wyclif sympathized with Langland).[1] Elizabeth Salter states the problem well when she says that "Langland criticism has found it possible to move between opposed, and not unreasonable conclusions — that he is at heart a reactionary, at heart a revolutionary" (Salter 1981, 108). In fact, the critics have been correct to see these positions in *Piers* and have been mistaken only to the extent that they have claimed for Langland a single position to the exclusion of others, for Langland was not interested in propounding a single comprehensive system. His subject would not allow it. One point that readers of *Piers* must constantly keep in mind is that Langland was a poet, not a theologian, not even a theological poet in the pattern of Dante. This is not to argue that poets can be less rigorous in their thought than theologians, that poetry is sloppier and less demanding than theology. It does mean, however, that poets do not necessarily think in terms of Aristotelian logic. Poetic logic operates according to other "rules"; and while it may consequently be less systematic, the results reflect more accurately the world that human beings inhabit. Salter again makes this point clearly: "No other poem of the alliterative tradition combines so distinctively rational procedure (in the verse paragraph, the individual speech or episode) with what appears, at first, to be a larger irrationality — an almost inconsequential attitude to the problem of developing and sustaining actions and arguments" (Salter 1969, 22).

This description of Langland's uniqueness need not be confined to the alliterative tradition, for *Piers* is, in many ways, a unique work. Gower may have entitled his work *Vox Clamantis*, but it was really Langland whose voice cried out in what he saw as the wilderness of the fourteenth century. Gower, writing out of understandable outrage and at conditions that must have seemed to him personally threatening, used easily recognizable models for his Latin poem. Langland, writing out of a different kind of outrage, a less personally threatened, more universal feeling, composed a different kind of poem, and it is his unique-ness that has often baffled readers, though his early audience seemed to know what he was about. It would help us to explain the poem's abrupt shifts in logic, in imagery, in time, and in space if we could discover the method and sources that help to make his poem unique. There have, of course, been many attempts in this direction that have contributed significantly to our understanding of the poem, but none has been completely successful. The problems in this area can be seen in the various attempts to define the poem's genre. Priscilla Martin writes of the "indistinctness of genre" and adds that "*Piers* employs, but hap-hazardly or as if they will not 'work', the forms of dream vision, debate, pilgrimage, encyclopaedic satire, psychomachia. Attempts to categorise the poem are hopeless: it is unlike anything else" (Martin 39). Similarly Daniel Murtaugh says, "Generic classification must prove a blind alley for a poem so intractably *sui generis*. One can call *Piers Plowman* a dream vision, a 'complaint,' a *consolatio*, a social satire, or any number of other things. All of these titles would fit tolerably well, but they would be appreciably less informative than the characterization of Wordsworth's Prelude as a Bildungsroman" (123). John Norton-Smith offers the opinion that "the overall 'idea' of the poem [is] beyond the application of any single, recognizable Classical, Late Antique or Medieval model" (126). One response is that of David Lawton, who says, "*Piers Plowman* is a maverick masterpiece which creates its own unique genre out of the very compendiousness, negatively of its satire and positively of its concerns . . ." (Lawton 1982, 10). Lawton's solution avoids the mistake of trying to force *Piers* into a genre in which it does not belong; but like Norton-Smith, Lawton mistakenly assumes that *Piers* is based on no "single, recognizable . . . model." Steven Justice, too, recognizes the problem of genre in *Piers Plowman*, and he asserts that "the *Visio's* pilgrimage to Truth is the search for a genre that will accommodate an authority neither abusive nor idiosyncratic" (291). While many of Justice's concerns with the poem are clearly justified, it is difficult to think of *Piers Plowman* as a quest for the appropriate genre. And Anne Middleton has written that "Unlike the works of Chaucer, which readily ac-knowledged their many debts to several 'maistres' in the classical and medieval literary tradition, *Piers Plowman* yields to 'sources and analogues' study little trace of its immediate literary antecedents and possible models..." (Middleton 1988, 19).

It will be the argument of the following study that in fact Langland did have, if not a specific model, at least a group of works that inspired him, that will account for many of the problems that have been mentioned, and that will help to explain other aspects of the poem as well. Those works, which include the many genres mentioned by Martin and Murtaugh, were the writings of the biblical prophets, especially Isaiah. *Piers Plowman*, in short, is a long poem that adopts the literary methods and forms of the biblical prophets as they were understood in the fourteenth century in order to address the problems of fourteenth-century England. The prophets may not be classifiable as "immediate literary antecedents," but they are, as I hope to show, of immediate importance in seeing how Langland's text works.

Of course there is nothing the slightest bit new about seeing a relationship between *Piers* and the prophets. Many readers have noticed the relationship and have used it in a variety of ways. Robertson and Huppé, for example, point out that in the first lines of the poem "the dreamer is clothed as if he were a 'shepe'; that is, he resembles the false prophets in sheep's clothing of the Gospel (Matt. 7.15)"(33). While Robertson and Huppé compare the dreamer to a false prophet, Robert W. Frank refers to the prophetic vision in order to deny that Langland used it: "The poet's artistic vision is moralistic rather than raptly prophetic, realistic rather than mystical" (118).

A common tendency in criticism has been to mention Langland's prophetic voice and then move on. Thus Derek Pearsall calls Langland "a missionary, a prophet, a voice crying in the wilderness," but his point is simply that as a consequence, "niceties of language as well as versification give way to the urgency of communicating his vision" (Pearsall 1977, 177), making it seem that neither the prophets nor Langland was concerned with the form of their messages. Edward Vasta offers a promising start when he says, "If we take 'prophet' in its Old Testament sense (excluding, of course, the notion of being divinely inspired) as designating those who prognosticate, record morally significant historical events, interpret the practices and institutions of this world as they are related to God's will, and urge contemporaries to moral and religious reform, the 'prophetic' character of Langland's mind is everywhere manifest in his poem. All the material found in *Piers Plowman* comes under these four ways in which the 'prophetic' mind operates, thus suggesting a unifying basis beneath the poem's seemingly digressionary contents" (13). Having said this, however, Vasta goes on to treat other matters.

Another tendency is to point to specific relationships between Langland and the prophets. For instance, Ames says, "Like the prophets, Langland believed that true religion consists in caring for the poor, the fatherless, the widowed, and the stranger" (11), and "Deeply imbued with the prophetic spirit, Langland rages against those who observe forms while ignoring the essence of the Law ..." (51). Like Vasta, Ames points to a vital aspect of the relationships, but she does not develop it. Other critics, like David Aers, see a connection between specific passages in *Piers* and in the prophets. Thus, in discussing lines 284-330 of Passus III (B-Text), Aers refers to Isaiah's picture of a messianic age (10). And David Fowler has discussed the prophetic aspects of the poem, especially the A-Text, although his discussion consists largely of references to specific lines from Amos or Isaiah that seem to have influenced Langland (chapter 4). Thus he is correct when he says that "this text offers itself to us as Scripture, as an extension of the Bible" (226), but it would have been helpful had he gone beyond specific line references for this reading. Barbara Nolan, too, recognizes some of the prophetic elements in *Piers Plowman* in her interesting discussion of the poem, but that discussion is flawed by her tendency to identify prophecy and apocalyptic (chapter 6), a subject to which I will return later.

Another approach is that of Morton Bloomfield, who treats the poem not merely in the tradition of apocalypse but actually as a fourteenth-century apocalypse. While the present study will differ from Bloomfield's work in a number of significant ways, Bloomfield's influence will frequently be obvious. For example, while Bloomfield stresses apocalyptic and monastic elements in the poem, this study will focus on more "worldly," societal elements; but there will be complete agreement with such statements as "Will wanders through this world to hear wonders, that is, to receive prophetic revelations" (69-70), for Will does indeed function in the same way as the biblical prophets, at least in the way that a fourteenth-century Christian poet could have understood the prophets as functioning. A central point of this study will be an elaboration of Bloomfield's assertion that "Langland speaks Bible" (37).

Finally, Stephen Barney has recently described the relationship between *Piers Plowman* and the prophetic writings. He briefly describes the prophets' tone and messages, their use of visions and difficult allusions, and their attitude toward the future, and he concludes, "If this fairly describes the prophetic stance and voice and theme, it likewise describes *Piers Plowman*. If its humor and wit distinguish the English poem's temper from the pure savage indignation of a prophetic book, still Langland's form and subject may most aptly be called prophetic. That *Piers* takes the form of a series of dream visions follows immediately from its prophetic character, and that it is allegorical is only a little less obviously a consequence of its prophetic manner of seeing" (Barney 1988, 119).

In the pages that follow, I shall examine the prophets themselves in some detail, how they might have been regarded in the fourteenth century, Langland's reasons for writing the poem as he did, and the implications of the prophetic background for understanding the poem. This examination will be rather lengthy, but it should have the effect of clarifying several aspects of *Piers Plowman*, among them the status of the dreamer-narrator, the emphasis in the poem on "common profit" and its relationship to individual salvation, the nature of the "quest" for Dowel (and its kin), Langland's manipulations of time and space, his use of biblical quotations, and, briefly, his relationship to other fourteenth-century poets. If this sounds like a great deal to cover, it is; but once we understand Langland's reliance on the prophets for his own inspiration, the rest quickly makes sense.

It must be emphasized again that the present study focuses on only a single aspect of *Piers Plowman*, namely Langland's use of the biblical prophets as his literary inspiration. Langland clearly made use of other sources, such as preaching, venality satire, anti-mendicant tracts, and others (many of which owe their own debt to the Bible); and if those sources seem neglected here, it is because so many of them have been treated so well elsewhere. But Langland's use of the prophets has a number of important implications for his poem, often casting new light on it as well as helping to reinforce some already existing views of the poem. Both functions, discovering new interpretations and reinforcing earlier ones, are important. The same goal can be reached by different paths, but the paths themselves are often worth closer examination. This is a study of one — certainly not the only — path.

Two final notes will close this introduction. The first involves biblical translations. Unless otherwise noted, all translations are from the Douay-Reims version, except that those biblical names that are most familiar in different versions will be given their more popular form. The second note concerns the text of the poem. This study will focus almost entirely on the C-Text, in the edition of Derek Pearsall. There are a number of reasons for choosing the C-Text. On the simplest level, it was Langland's last version, the one that expressed his latest thoughts. We cannot know, of course, any details about the "publication" of the earlier versions and so it is foolish to offer any conjectures. Did Langland intend them for public reading? Did he, like John Fowles with *The Magus*, reconsider what he had written? Was he, like Henry James, someone who could not look at his work without revising it? We do not know. The numerous attempts at understanding the changes that Langland made from version to version have had to face the kind of difficulties that E.T. Donaldson describes in his discussion of Langland's language. On the one hand he says that in C the poet has replaced figurative language by flat statement, "an alteration that results in the C-text's appearing, at times, more philosophic than poetic." On the other hand, "At other times C's tendency to get away from the concrete and visual into the abstract and ideal betrays itself in his choice, as between two concrete words, of the vague one over the more definite" (51-52). In other words, C is simultaneously less figurative and less definite. Clearly something is different in C's language, but it is difficult to pinpoint just what that may be. The key, perhaps, can be found in some of Langland's other changes, many of which will be discussed in what follows, particularly in the additions that Langland made to the C-Text — like the autobiographical passage in Passus V and his extra attention to minstrels — and deletions — like the tearing of the pardon. These changes, and probably the alterations in the language as well, are the result of Langland's increasing willingness to present his work as a species of prophecy, which, as we shall see, is especially evident in the C-Text. Langland began his work in loose imitation of the prophets, focusing primarily on their message, but in the twenty or so tumultuous years that separated A and C, his sense of his own rightness, and the necessity to speak out, increased, and he understood more and more his own prophetic role, resulting in the C-Text. To see how this process developed, let us begin with the prophets.

II. The Prophets

1. THE PROPHETS IN THEIR TIME

Delbert Hillers has written, "The books of Israel's prophets are among the most difficult in the Old Testament, and probably among the most difficult books ever written. The oracles are often tantalizingly brief and are for the most part couched in a highly concentrated poetic language and joined together with no obvious regard for logical or chronological sequence. The reader . . . is often at a loss to tell where an individual speech begins or ends . . ." (124). Given the kind of difficulties Hillers describes, it is not surprising that interpretations of the prophetic books have varied so greatly. The following pages represent an attempt to present certain aspects of the prophets that are important for *Piers Plowman* and to explain how and why Langland used them. It might be noticed, at the start, that with only a few modifications, Hillers' description of the prophets could apply equally well to *Piers*.

Although the literary prophets, those prophets to whom specific books of the Bible are attributed, wrote over a span of more than five centuries, they are united by a variety of themes and techniques. It should be remembered that the Church numbered David among the prophets, as well. Nicholas of Lyra, to choose only one example out of many, noted that "Although the book of Psalms is included among the holy writings (*agiographia*) by the Jews, among the Latins it is placed in the category of prophetic books" (Minnis 1988, 271). The reason for this placement was expressed in English by the translators of the Wyclif Bible in their prologue to Psalms, which largely comes from Jerome: "This book Sauter is clepid, that is to seie, the book of songis of Dauith, and of Asaph . . . wherynne is conteyned profesie of the comynge of Crist, of his birthe, and of his power and teching; of his passioun and his rising aȝen fro deeth, and of his ascensioun and of his comynge aȝen in the laste doom ..." (II.736). As we shall see, this passage represents one form of prophecy as it was considered in the Middle Ages; such Christological readings can also be found in the other prophets. Furthermore, Langland clearly used Psalms to a great extent in such episodes as that involving the Four Daughters of God, and quoted from them copiously; a study of Langland and the Psalter could be quite valuable. However, because Langland was primarily influenced by the Major Prophets, especially Isaiah, this examination will focus on those prophets who prophesied between the eighth and sixth centuries B.C.

The historical books of the Bible, especially Kings and Chronicles, on which someone like Langland would have relied for his knowledge of biblical history, are not historical in a modern sense, reflecting, as they often do, the history from the point of view of the prophets. They do, however, describe, probably accurately, the period of prophetic activity in which we are interested as a time of religious, political, and social turmoil. It must be understood, though, that the division into categories like religious, political, and social is artificial, for the prophets regarded them all as reflections of a single, divine standard of order. A disturbance in one area inevitably disturbed the order in the others. In the ritual sphere, for example, the prophets' constant complaint is that the people have abandoned God and God's laws and that they are worshipping other, worthless gods. The result of this unfaithfulness, often described in terms of adultery, is that morality has disintegrated, as can be seen in the collapse of social life, most obviously in the callous attitude of the society toward the poor. And of course this weakened morality is reflected in the behavior of the rulers, who oppress their own people and who seek to ensure their safety by making political alliances with other rulers rather than by relying on God. Because these areas are so interrelated, however, the scheme can be presented in a number of other ways: The social collapse contributes to the political and ritual collapse, or the political collapse leads to the social and ritual collapse. In fact the order is not important, because the problem is not really one of cause and effect, and reforming one area will not automatically bring about reform in the others. Furthermore, the problem is complicated by the question of individual and communal responsibility: The flaws of the individual contribute to the failure of the society, and the failure of the society encourages the corruption of the individual, so that reform must address both the individual and the community. What is needed is a complete transformation of the society and of the individuals who comprise that society, a restoration of proper order in all the areas of the society. There were attempts at such restoration, under King Josias, for example; but generally the kings in both the northern kingdom of Israel (conquered by Assyria in 720 B.C.) and in the southern kingdom of Judah (conquered by Babylonia in 586 B.C.) are described as a bad lot, with the last years of Judah, dominated by the vicious fifty-five year reign of Manasses (4 Kings 21), especially bad. And what made Judah's crimes even worse was that

Judah should have learned from the example of Israel, which had already been destroyed for its sins. It is against this background, from just before Israel's destruction until just after Judah's, that the prophets with whom we are concerned delivered their prophecies. We must keep in mind that the prophets, however universal their messages, were addressing specific problems in their society. In fact, the universal aspect of those messages may merely indicate how little progress society has made in the last three millennia.

The questions of what the prophets did and how they did it date from the time of the prophets themselves and, perhaps because of the diversity among the prophets, have never been fully answered. Nonetheless, there are certain generalizations that we can safely make. One of the most important points to emphasize is that the prophets were not simply people who could read the future. As Levi Olan says, "The Hebrew prophets were not soothsayers; some of their predictions about particular events never took place. The Medes did not destroy Babylon as Jeremiah had predicted, and Cyrus never became a worshipper of Yahwe as Deutero-Isaiah had foretold. The validity of the prophet's message did not depend upon the fulfillment of his prediction of a particular event at a given time and place" (xii). Although Olan is essentially correct, his position is somewhat complicated by the words of Deuteronomy 18:25, "Whatsoever that same prophet foretelleth in the name of the Lord, and it cometh not to pass: that thing the Lord hath not spoken, but the prophet hath forged it by the pride of his mind: and therefore thou shalt not fear him."

There are a number of ways to reconcile these apparently contradictory approaches. One that was popular in earlier times was to claim that the seemingly unfulfilled prophecies were allegorical and that consequently the prophecies really had been fulfilled. Another, and for us more relevant way, is to recognize that the prophets were people who could not read the future but who could read the present and make predictions based on that. Such predictions were always conditional. They always contain an unstated clause that says something like, "If you continue to behave as you have been behaving . . ." followed by the prediction. The focus of their revelation was not what would happen in the future but rather that their people were behaving badly, were violating the ritual or, more often, the moral teachings of their religion and that unless they repented and reformed, returned to the practices that had been prescribed for them, they would be punished. Their point was reform, not prediction. (Langland, to look ahead for a moment, makes this point in III.328 when he says, "So god gyueth nothyng þat *si* ne is the glose.")

We can see this theme quite clearly by looking at one of the least typical biblical prophets, Jonah. Like many other prophets, Jonah was reluctant to adopt the role that God had assigned him; but Jonah, unlike Isaiah, Jeremiah, and Ezekiel, actually attempted to flee from that mission, largely because he misunderstood that mission, which was to make the inhabitants of Nineveh repent. Jonah did not understand that when he was told to preach, his proclamation, "Yet forty days and Nineveh shall be destroyed" (3:4), automatically contained the "prophetic conditional" — that is, the whole prophecy should read, "If you continue to behave as you have been behaving, yet forty days and Nineveh shall be destroyed." The non-fulfillment of Jonah's prediction seems, according to the Deuteronomist, to make Jonah a false prophet. This, in fact, is Jonah's point at the end of the book: he appears to be a false prophet because his prediction has not come true, and he clearly identifies prophecy with prediction. The actual fact is, however, that the book of Jonah presents one of the very few instances in the Bible of successful prophecy, precisely because the prediction did not come true, for the function of the prophet is not to foretell but to "forthtell," to point out sin and urge repentance. Consequently, the predictions have to be understood correctly before we can tell if they have come true.

More to the point is Jeremiah's argument that one way of telling whether a prophet is true or false is to see if he praises or condemns. If a prophet says that what he sees is good, he is not a true prophet: "For from the least of them even to the greatest, all are given to covetousness: and from the prophet even to the priest, all are guilty of deceit. And they healed the breach of the daughter of my people disgracefully, saying: Peace, peace: and there was no peace" (6:13-14). It is the false prophets who overlook corruption and who proclaim peace when there is no peace. Against a background of corruption and collapse, the true prophets offered a way for the people to avoid calamity, but it meant telling the people the truth, telling them what they had done wrong. And the people seldom listened, except to what they wanted to hear.

The prophets, then, were raising challenging questions — and providing some answers — but the people wanted reassurances and fortune telling. As Yehezkel Kaufmann has written, "The lasting value of the prophets resides in the noble religious and moral ideas to which they gave voice. The people, however, set equal store by their mantic powers. Generations of believers searched the biblical prophets for allusions to contemporary and future events" (353). There have always been readers who recognized the "noble religious and moral ideas" of the prophets, but those ideas are, as we shall see, simultaneously so simple and so difficult, so reactionary and so revolutionary, that it has been more convenient to behave as though the prophets were really saying something else. In the simplest possible terms the main thrust of the prophets' message can be summarized in the words of Isaiah 1:16-17, which I quote from the Wyclif Bible so that we can see a fourteenth-century reading of the passage: "Be ȝee washen, beth clene; taketh awei the euel of ȝoure thoȝtes fro myn eȝen; resteth to do shreudely, lerneth to do wel. Secheth dom, helpeth to the opressid, demeth to the faderles child, defendeth the widewe" (III.228). Repent, learn to do well, and then do it. The task is as easy, and as difficult, as that. Despite the simplicity of the words, "do well" is as difficult a concept for Isaiah as it is for Langland.

There is ample precedent in the Bible for Isaiah's formulation.[1] The laws of the Torah (a word often mistakenly translated as "Law" rather than "Teaching") can be divided into the categories of ritual and moral laws. This division is obvious in the Ten Commandments, especially in the Jewish system of counting the Commandments. Those Commandments on the first tablet, such as "Thou shalt not have strange gods before me" or "Remember that thou keep holy the sabbath day" are of a ritual nature, that is, they are between human beings and God. Those Commandments on the second tablet, such as "Thou shalt not commit adultery" and "Thou shalt not steal," are of a moral nature, that is, they govern the relationships among human beings. This division, which can be applied to most of the laws of the Torah, clear though it may seem, is artificial and the source of all sorts of errors. A different approach would make the point that the Commandments, and the two realms that they seem to represent, are intricately bound up with each other, that they are inseparable. The proper performance of the ritual laws should serve as a constant reminder of our moral obligations; and the fulfillment of those moral obligations is evidence of our full understanding of the ritual laws.

Surely this is the point that Jesus makes when he responds to the question, "Which is the greatest commandment in the law?" Jesus' response is to quote the profession of faith from Deuteronomy 6:5, "Thou shalt love the Lord thy God with thy whole heart, and with thy whole soul, and with thy whole mind." But then Jesus makes a significant addition, citing Leviticus 19:18: "This is the greatest and the first commandment. And the second is like to this: Thou shalt love thy neighbour as thyself. On these two commandments dependeth the whole law and the prophets" (Matthew 22:36-40). Jesus has cited two commandments, one concerning human-divine relationships and one concerning purely human relationships, and has said that they are like each other. Again we see the intimate connection between the ritual and moral realms.

Unfortunately, as Jesus and the prophets make clear, it is far too easy to make the artificial division between the ritual and moral realms. Even if ritual laws — sacrifices, dietary laws, or holiday rites in the Bible; prayer, fasts, and confession in the Middle Ages — seem oppressive, they are relatively easy. They can be carried out by memorizing the rules and mechanically going through the processes. No observer can measure the sincerity that informs such ritual obedience, but everyone can see that the ritual has been performed. The rules are clear. But moral laws are different. The rules are not so clear, and the performance of moral laws often involves us in making decisions about complicated questions of right and wrong. Furthermore, moral laws frequently require us to make personal sacrifices, to control our acquisitive urges, and to be fair to people we may not like; and even if we carry out these laws, there is a good chance that no one will know we have. Thus the moral laws are much more difficult to obey, and a constant complaint of the prophets is that the people obey the ritual but not the moral laws. Again the first chapter of Isaiah is a good example, particularly the verse just before the ones we cited above: "To what purpose do you offer me the multitude of your victims, saith the Lord? I am full, I desire not holocausts of rams, and fat of fatlings, and blood of calves, and lambs, and buck goats. . . . Offer sacrifices no more in vain. . . . My soul hateth your new moons, and your solemnities: they are become troublesome to me, I am weary of bearing them. And when you stretch forth your hands, I will turn away my eyes from you: and when you multiply prayer, I will not hear: for your hands are full of blood" (Isaiah 1:11-15). Empty observance of the ritual laws, which implies a false profession of faith, constitutes a violation of both the ritual and moral laws. One cannot serve God without serving other people. Therefore, says Isaiah, "lerneth to do wel"; and the examples he gives, seeking justice and caring for the weak, stand in sharp contrast to the elaborate but misguided sacrifices that the prophet has condemned. Human beings have social responsibilities, but these social responsibilities have a divine dimension.

We can see this point illustrated in the Gospels as well, when Jesus tells the rich young man who wants "life everlasting" and who claims to have kept the commandments, "If thou wilt be perfect, go sell what thou hast, and give to the poor, and thou shalt have treasure in heaven: and come follow me" (Matthew 19:21). Here again social responsibility is stressed, but this story illustrates another aspect of the topic, the relationship between the individual and the community. Jesus here promises the young man individual salvation as a reward for his service to the community. Similarly, Isaiah, while he does not mention individual salvation, at least on a literal level, gives much attention to the welfare of the community, as do the other prophets. J. Lindblom has even argued that "The subject of the prophetic religion is in the first place the people as a community" (308). The punishment that the people will suffer for their sins at the hands of the Babylonians, for instance, will not affect only those citizens who have done wrong. The entire community will be held responsible. Herein lies one answer to a common problem in theodicy: why do the good suffer along with the bad? The answer that the prophets give is that every person in a society is responsible for doing well and will prosper or suffer to the extent that the society prospers or suffers. Each individual is responsible for his or her own actions, but each individual is also a part of society and is responsible for that society. Again, it is not possible to have a relationship with God that omits other human beings. As James Word has said in discussing Hosea, "God's relationship to Israel is at once communal and intimately personal. It comprehends the interior dimensions of human existence — man's reason, will, and affections — as well as the social dimension of his corporate life. God is the Lord of Israel, the people of the covenant, and he is the Lord of each man's personal destiny. He can be Lord of each only by being Lord of both. This is a fundamental conviction of the biblical writers" (8). The relationships in a society must contain a divine element, which brings us back to the inseparability of moral and ritual observances.

What the prophets, as well as other parts of the Bible, present, then, is a blueprint for a utopia in which people are responsible for themselves and for their society and in which they recognize that those areas of responsibility coincide. Of course, because we are flawed, that blueprint has never really been used. It demands more from us than we may be capable of delivering, which explains why people over the centuries have been more interested in reading the prophets for their alleged predictions than for learning about "the noble religious and moral ideas to which they gave voice." What Kierkegaard said about the New Testament is equally applicable to the Old:

> Suppose that in the New Testament it were written, for example (a thing which we can at least suppose), that every man should have $100,000 . . . do you believe that then there would be any question of a commentary? — or not rather that everyone would say: That is easy enough to understand, there is absolutely no need of a commentary, for God's sake, let us be delivered from any commentary . . .

> But what actually is written in the New Testament (about the narrow way, about dying to the world) is not a bit more difficult to understand than that about the $100,000. The difficulty lies elsewhere, in the fact that it is not to our liking — and therefore, therefore we must have commentaries and professors and commentaries.

> It is to get rid of doing God's will that we have invented learning . . . we shield ourselves by hiding behind tomes.
> (Forrester 122)

The ideals are there, clearly stated, but, says Kierkegaard, they are so difficult to perform that we have invented system after system to get around them, to say that they mean something else or that in pursuing our own selfish goals we are somehow fulfilling the ideals. The prophetic books, like the New Testament (and like *Piers Plowman*), are aware of such casuistry and reject it outright. Isaiah says, "Lerneth to do wel." It is not enough just to know what "wel" is: we must also learn to "do" it. And having learned, we must then actually do it. The task is that easy — and that difficult. It is, as it looks back to old values, that reactionary; and it is, as it seeks to reform society, that revolutionary. "Lerneth to do wel." It is an order that some people, like Langland, have taken seriously.

Because the prophets were so deeply concerned with the ideals to be pursued by the individual and the society, because they were interested in establishing a righteous kingdom on earth, it should not be surprising that they played a part in the political life of Israel. We see numerous examples in the prophetic books of prophets addressing kings and of kings either addressing or condemning the prophets. Isaiah in particular delivered his prophecies directly to the kings. In fact, the connection between kings and prophets was even closer than at first appears. As Joseph Blenkinsopp explains, the title "Servant of God," which was originally applied to Moses, the prophet and political leader of the Israelites, was later used to describe both prophets and kings, since "the monarchy was also charged with the task of mediation, prophecy and monarchy being viewed as parallel embodiments of the mediatorial function and charismatic office of Moses. . . . By the time of the exile, then, the parallelism between prophecy and monarchy as executors of the divine will and mediators between God and the people was well established" (215).[2] Generally, of course, the realities of political life led the prophets to rebuke the kings, which resulted in the imprisonment of Jeremiah, for example. In addition, the prophets, even when, like Jeremiah, they were from priestly families, did not hesitate to attack the priests for corrupting the religion, either by allowing the worship of other gods or by encouraging the practice of empty religion. Religious, political, and moral problems were all evidence of the same problems for the prophets, problems that they were forced to confront.

Exactly how and why the prophets were forced to confront these problems is itself a problem. Jeremiah's agony at being a prophet is well known: "For I am speaking now this long time crying out against iniquity . . . and the word of the Lord is made a reproach to me, and a derision all the day. Then I said: I will not make mention of him, nor speak any more in his name: and there came in my heart as a burning fire, shut up in my bones, and I was wearied, not being able to bear it" (20:8-9). The prophet is compelled to speak by some force that he cannot subdue: "My bowels, my bowels are in pain, the senses of my heart are troubled within me, I will not hold my peace, for my soul hath heard the sound of the trumpet, the cry of battle" (Jeremiah 4:19). Even when the feeling is not quite so dramatic, it is inescapable: "The lion shall roar, who will not fear? The Lord God hath spoken, who shall not prophesy?" (Amos 3:8). The assumption of the prophets is that the words are not their own, however individualized they may seem to us. "The true prophets are conscious of being mouthpieces of Yahweh and nothing else. They are nothing but channels for the stream of revelation. What they have to bring forth is not their own words (they would be worthless), but only the precious divine word which has been put in their mouth" (Lindblom 114). We can see these ideas in those chapters that describe the calls to prophecy of Isaiah, Jeremiah, and Ezekiel.

All of the Major Prophets provide detailed descriptions of their calls to prophecy, descriptions that in many ways characterize the individual prophets, though they share certain motifs as well. Thus, each of them is characterized by an initial unwillingness to be a prophet, a motif that perhaps has its source in Moses' experience at the burning bush, when he invents excuse after excuse not to be God's messenger. As a result, one sign of the true prophet became humility in the face of God's commands, a feeling of unworthiness. Jeremiah, for example, speaks with God in very human terms; and his response to God's choice of him as a prophet is "Ah, ah, ah, Lord God: behold, I cannot speak, for I am a child" (1:6). But then "the Lord put forth his hand, and touched my mouth: and the Lord said to me: Behold I have given my words in thy mouth" (1:9), after which he begins to have visions and to declare them publicly. Similarly, Ezekiel is overwhelmed by his vision of the Divine Chariot, but he is told to "open thy mouth, and eat what I give thee. And I looked, and behold, a hand was sent to me, wherein was a book rolled up: and he spread it before me, and it was written within and without: and there were written in it lamentations, and canticles, and woe" (2:8-9). Finally Isaiah, who, as will be seen, exerted the greatest influence on Langland, received his initiation into prophecy by having his mouth touched with a live coal, so that, purified, he could respond to the divine question "Whom shall I send? and who shall go for us?" with "Lo, here am I, send me" (6:6-8). Each of these prophets is called by some action involving the mouth, emphasizing the divine origin of their messages.

Of course this notion raises yet another problem that will be most important for our consideration of *Piers Plowman*: do the prophets simply repeat the exact words that God has put into their mouths, or are they somehow responsible for the forms those words take? To what extent have the prophets shaped their words? Stephen Geller, in an article aptly titled "Were the Prophets Poets?," states the problem succinctly: "A prophet is . . . the mouthpiece of a god. A poet is a 'maker,' a craftsman in words. The former is a medium, the latter an artist. A prophet who consciously molded his prophecy would be false. A poet whose verse did not reflect his personality would be no true artist" (211). Certain books of the Bible, such as Psalms, Lamentations, Job, and others, have traditionally been considered poetic, but the controversy over the poetic status of the prophets has ancient roots. The third-century *Didascalia Apolstolorum* forbade the reading of pagan literature but suggested, "If you wish to read histories, take those of the Book of Kings: if you want poetry and wisdom, take the Prophets . . . if you desire songs, you have the Psaltery" (Kugel 151). On the other hand, Jerome, who laid out his translation of the prophets in verse form, warned in his preface to Isaiah (in the fourteenth-century translation), "No man, whan the profetes he shal seen with versis to ben discriued, in metre eyme he hem anent the Ebrues to ben bounden, and any thing lic to han of Salmes, or of the werkus of Salomon. . ." (III.224). Parts of the prophets are undeniably poetic, such as Isaiah 5, which declares itself in the first verse to be "canticle," but otherwise Jerome denies the poetic status of the prophetic writings.

Over the centuries this controversy continued. A popular exercise was the attempt, necessarily unsuccessful, to describe the meter of biblical poetry in terms that belonged to Latin and Greek poetry. Despite the futility of such exercises, the notion persisted that prophets and poets were related. Nonetheless, for those who believed that the prophetic messages were dictated by God, the idea that the prophets were poets was most troublesome.

As Kugel's work illustrates, the controversy continues even now, though most critics recognize the poetic aspect of prophetic literature: "In prophecy an ostensibly divine message is contained in a human medium. A message of personal, national, or occasionally cosmic importance must be conveyed in language which is composed in an aesthetic construction" (Friedman 11). Langland, who considered himself a poet and who adopted a prophetic stance, would have found a precedent for this combination in the prophets themselves: "Sometimes the prophets chose to appear as poets or minstrels rather than speakers or preachers" (Lindblom 154, citing Isaiah 5, Amos 5, and Ezekiel 14, 19, 27, and 32).

What concerns us now is that whether or not the prophets were considered to be poets either in their own time or by later readers, their works clearly contain a variety of what we would now call literary genres. Lindblom's enumeration of the rhetorical and literary modes in the prophets is instructive: he cites

> exhortations to repentance, reproaches, announcements of judgment, threats against the apostates in Israel and against pagan nations, words of consolation and promises for the future. There are woe and satire, scorn and lamentation, hymns and prayers, monologues and dialogues, judicial debating, utterances formulated after a ritual pattern, description of visions and auditions and confessions of personal experiences of different kinds. There are letters and messages, short oracles and extended sermons, historical retrospects, confessions of sin, decisions in cultic matters, parables and allegories, similes and sententious phrases of wisdom, lyric poetry of various kinds and discussions of religious and moral problems.
>
> (Lindblom 155)

As we saw earlier, critics have pointed out the same variety of literary modes in *Piers Plowman* and have found this variety an impediment in their attempts to classify the poem. Bloomfield has thus far provided the best understanding of the poem's form by showing how it "is based on three literary genres: the allegorical dream narrative; the dialogue, *consolatio*, or debate; and the encyclopedic (or Menippean) satire. And it is influenced by three religious genres (or forms): the complaint, the commentary, and the sermon" (10). All of these Bloomfield finds subsumed in the apolcalyptic. It seems more accurate, in view of the tendency in the prophets and in *Piers* to rely on so many — and so many of the same — modes, to see Langland reflecting prophetic practice.

The variety of literary modes is one of the elements that has made the prophetic books seem so confusing even to modern readers who realize that these books are actually anthologies, collections of various prophetic utterances. There is another prophetic technique that seems strange to us but must have seemed perfectly normal when the prophets wrote. As Kaufmann explains, "There is never a succession of scenes; the vision stands alone, and is followed by the word which the prophet is charged to convey to men" (348-49). Consequently, even when we are dealing with an extended section by a single prophet, there is little sense of continuity. Instead episode follows episode, cumulatively building effects by means of juxtaposition rather than through narrative unity. Thus even Kaufmann, who argues for the unity of Isaiah 1-39, is forced to admit, "The book of Isaiah is generally regarded as the most composite and disordered of the prophetic books" (379). Whether or not biblical scholars can demonstrate the unity of these chapters, they certainly appear disordered, and it is that appearance that is our concern, for while we may now attribute the disorder to such factors as multiple authorship, medieval readers saw the book as a unified whole, the work of a single author and part of that larger unified whole, the Bible; and they found ways to demonstrate that unity. What appear to us as irregularities in chronological or spatial relationships were accepted and internalized, as we shall see.

Despite such narrative disorder and despite internal contradictions, there are clear unities of theme, purpose, and technique in these remarkable works. The prophets' task, which they regarded as a burden, was to transform the individuals and the society that they addressed, to bring their people back to a proper appreciation of and relationship with God so that order would be restored in the world, thereby benefitting both the individuals and the society. Blenkinsopp summarizes the effects of the prophetic books well when he says, "No writings in the Scriptures more than these confront us so directly with the reality of God or force us so inescapably to question the mundane and even the religious perceptions that tend to control our lives" (18). The prophetic books may not be systematic theological treatises, but they do force us to consider moral and theological problems, which, again, they do not regard as separable. It should, in addition, be noted that the prophets themselves were full of doubts, as we can see in their respective calls to prophecy. Large sections of Jeremiah, especially, express the prophet's uncertainties about himself and about God's way of ruling the world (e.g., Jeremiah 12:1: "Thou indeed, O Lord, art just, if I plead with thee, but yet I will speak what is just to thee: Why doth the way of the wicked prosper: why is it well with them that transgress, and do wickedly?"). If the prophets have such doubts about human and divine behavior, how much the more should their readers have them!

These prophetic doubts also clarify another facet of the prophets, one that can best be expressed in negative terms. The prophets are emphatically not mystical and, with the exception of a few chapters, they are not apocalyptic. The method by which the prophets received their messages from God has already been mentioned in relation to prophetic initiations, and what we saw there is true throughout their writings: In some way God speaks to the prophets, tells them what to say or shows them visions, but the prophets never speak of losing their identity or their self-hood, of being absorbed in the Godhead. Quite to the contrary, the prophets maintain a remarkable degree of self-possession when God calls to them, and their very unwillingness to take on the prophetic role bespeaks their strong sense of otherness. The prophets may present themselves as confused, inquisitive, indignant, or overwhelmed, but they are never in less than full control of themselves.

The case of apocalypticism is slightly different. There are apocalyptic chapters in the prophetic books, though not nearly so many as medieval readers were likely to think. Even so, those apocalyptic chapters were intended to offer the people comfort, to indicate that after the promised punishment there would be a restoration, so that even if the present audience would not repent, the proper relationship between God and the world would be re-established. As Kaufmann explains, such chapters do not make the prophets apocalyptic: "The distinctive feature of apocalypse is its anxious inquiry and research into the secrets of the cosmos. The literary prophet, on the other hand, is first of all a messenger whose task is not to reveal hidden things, but to command or reprove in the name of God. To be sure, he is privy to 'the secrets' of God; he knows and reveals the future; he sees visions and symbols and interprets them. Yet all these are subordinate to his message and his mission" (348). Certainly some ages adopt a more apocalyptic outlook than others, and so lay greater stress on the apocalyptic chapters in the prophets; but clearly Kaufmann is correct in seeing those as subordinate. If the prophets "reveal" anything, it is the people's wickedness and the way to repentance, along with the threat of punishment. Of course that message requires some amount of effort on the part of the people: they must learn to do well, which is hardly as exciting as apocalyptic speculation. In addition, people would obviously rather hear that what they are doing is fine and that, at least for them, things will continue to be fine. Apparently the people of ancient Israel and Judah heard that message, which explains the sometimes obsessive concern of the prophets with false prophets.

A good example of a false prophet can be found in Jeremiah 28, where Hananias tells the people that all will be fine. Such a prediction would surely have made him a popular man, more popular, certainly, than Jeremiah. The problem was how to know whether a prophet was a false prophet. Deuteronomy, as we saw earlier, said that we should see whether a prophet's prophecies come true. This test was clearly inadequate, as we can see in Jeremiah's response to Hananias: "Amen, the Lord so do: the Lord perform thy words, which thou hast prophesied. . . . Nevertheless hear this word that I speak in thy ears, and in the ears of all the people: . . . The prophet that prophesied peace: when his word shall come to pass, the prophet shall be known, whom the Lord hath sent in truth" (28:6-9). In short, when a prophet tells the people good things, they must wait until those things happen to determine whether he is a true prophet. Jeremiah provides no such test for a prophet who rebukes and condemns. Apparently such a prophet is to be taken more seriously. This judgment applies equally well to prophets who deal with moral behavior or with future events, including those false prophets who looked forward eagerly to some apocalyptic time in which, they preached, their people would be vindicated. To such prophets Amos said, "Woe to them that desire the day of the Lord" (5:18). And Isaiah added, "O my people, they that call thee blessed, the same deceive thee, and destroy the way of thy steps" (3:12). False prophets like Hananias — and they must have been plentiful — encouraged the people's immorality by assuring them that everything was in order. It was the job of real prophets like Jeremiah to show that things were in disorder and to illustrate what true order meant.

The argument between Hananias and Jeremiah illustrates another aspect of the prophets: they were preachers, that is, they delivered oral discourses attacking the sins of the people and offering direction on the necessity and methods of repentance. While many of their prophecies were directed at specific audiences — kings, priests, other individuals or groups — others were intended for a general audience of the people. In Jeremiah 36, for example, Jeremiah, at God's instructions, commands Baruch to write down the prophecies he has delivered. That this act was important enough to be recorded reminds us that the prophets lived in a largely oral culture. Furthermore, preaching had a long, traditional history in Israel. Almost the whole of Deuteronomy is a series of sermons delivered by Moses in a style that E. W. Nicholson describes as "verbose and repetitious . . . which points for its origin not to the pen of an author — as a literary style it would have to be judged amongst the poorest in the Old Testament — but to the lips of a preacher or teacher who was vitally concerned with impressing the urgency of his message upon the minds and consciences of those who listened" (7). The sermons that comprise Deuteronomy may not be like the sermons of Augustine or Bernard, but they are clearly religious exhortations delivered by Moses to a potentially wayward people. If the prophetic writings are more poetic and show a greater sense of style, they nevertheless originated as sermons preached to the people with a sense of great urgency before the anticipated disaster and may have served as models for later sermons.

These, then, are the characteristics of the prophetic works that concern us most for a study of *Piers Plowman*: the close ties established among the religious, political, and moral realms, with an emphasis on the moral; the major purpose of bringing about repentance so that order can be re-established in the world and disasters can be avoided; the prophets' descriptions of their calls; the condemnation of false prophets; the apparent disorder of many of the prophetic writings; and the poetic aspect of those writings. This last element, involving such topics as the nature of prophetic imagery, the use of allegory, the descriptions of visions, and the use of narrative, must now be addressed.

2. THE PROPHET AS POET

One problem in reading the prophets, as we have seen, is the apparent disorder of many of their utterances. Words, lines, verses, and images often seem out of place or unnecessary. Transitions are frequently missing, so that we jump from one image or one thought to another with startling abruptness. One explanation may be the piecemeal composition and redaction of the texts, especially Isaiah; and another may involve the late date at which these ancient writings were divided into chapters and verses. Since neither of these explanations was available to medieval readers, they are irrelevant for our purposes. Instead we must look at the prophetic works as they were received and, as much as possible, perceived by earlier readers, especially those aspects of the prophets that are relevant for a study of *Piers Plowman*. The point of the following rather lengthy discussion of prophetic poetry is to indicate how the prophets used literary techniques to convey and to reinforce their messages. Later I will try to show how Langland was influenced by these techniques, but for now it is worth remembering that Langland has been described as having "no apparent care for the minutiae of craftsmanship" (Kane 234-35) or as lacking "literary or artistic skill" (Norton-Smith 126), arguments which could also be made about the prophetic writings. Furthermore, it is likely that the prophetic writings (including the Psalms) constituted the best poetry that Langland had available to him. My argument will be that Langland not only considered himself a poet but that he really was a poet and that he often wrote in a style similar to that used by the prophets. This is another way in which, to use Bloomfield's phrase, Langland "speaks Bible. . . . His whole mind is steeped in the Bible; it is a real language for him" (37).[3]

The first chapter of Isaiah provides a good example of prophetic poetry. Here we read:

> 4. Woe to the sinful nation, a people laden with iniquity, a wicked seed, ungracious children: they have forgotten the Lord. . . 5. For what shall I strike you any more, you that increase transgression? the whole head is sick, and the whole heart is sad. 6. From the sole of the foot unto the top of the head, there is no soundness therein: wounds and bruises and swelling sores: they are not bound up, nor dressed nor

fomented with oil. 7. Your land is desolate, your cities are
burnt with fire: your country strangers devour before your
face, and it shall be desolate as when wasted by enemies. 8.
And the daughter of Sion shall be left as a covert in a
vineyard, and as a lodge in a garden of cucumbers, and as a
city that is laid waste.

This piling on of images has its source partially, at least, in the prophet's anger,
which leads him to castigate the people in a variety of ways; but it also originates
in a specific biblical poetic style known as parallelism. As James Kugel describes
it, "The parallelistic style in the Bible consists not of stringing together clauses
that bear some semantic, syntactic, or phonetic resemblance, nor yet of 'saying
the same thing twice.'" Rather it is a style in which the second half of the line
both continues the first half and yet is separated from it in "a typically emphatic,
'seconding' style" (53). We can see this style in Isaiah's use of imagery. The
images in 1:4-8 are not disparate expressions of the prophet's anger, although
they may appear so. They are, instead, complementary. Verse 4 begins with
Isaiah calling Israel "a sinful nation," as straightforward a phrase as we are likely
to find. He then moves to a metaphoric plane when he calls it "a people laden
with iniquity." This is not merely a restatement of the first phrase. It illustrates
that phrase; it gives us almost a visual perception of that first phrase. Then Israel
becomes "a wicked seed, ungracious children." "Wicked" is straightforward but
vague. In what way are they wicked? By being ungracious. Furthermore, the
nation has suddenly become "seed" and "children." Whose children? The
Lord's. By yoking these images together, the prophet has not simply said the
same thing in five different ways. Instead he has intensified his condemnation,
establishing that the people of Israel are God's children whose ungraciousness,
wicked in itself, has led them to be sinful, laden with iniquity. As Robert Alter
says in explaining why the prophets used verse, "It was not just for the
memorability of poetic language or for the sense that poetry was a medium of
elevated and perhaps solemn discourse but also because this poetic vehicle of
parallelistic verse offered a particularly effective way of imaginatively realizing
inevitability, of making powerfully manifest to the listener the idea that consequences he might choose not to contemplate could happen, would happen,
would happen without fail" (76).

At this point the prophet abruptly shifts to a whole new metaphor that
describes Israel as a body that is sick and wounded. This metaphor, unlike those
in verse 4, is carried through two verses and almost becomes a minor allegory,
describing the rottenness of the country. It also continues the movement from
nation to children that began in verse 4 by now comparing the entire nation to
an individual, thereby helping to focus the earlier images more clearly and to
hint at the relationship between the individual and the society. Verses 5 and 6
complement verse 4 by means of thematic continuity, made more striking by the

juxtaposition of metaphors. This juxtaposition continues in verse 7, which begins with another clear statement, "Your land is desolate." This phrase marks a transition from the body metaphor back to the nation, providing an application of the metaphor from the previous two verses by implying the comparison between desolated land and desolated body and focusing the audience's attention on the specific problem of an invading army. (It is likely that this prophecy was delivered during a siege, possibly that of Sennacherib in 701 B.C.) Strangers devour the country and it will be wasted.

After these bleak words, we hear of the daughter of Sion. This metaphor returns us to the ungrateful children of verse 4 and the individual person of verses 5 and 6. This daughter of Sion will be left "as a covert in a vineyard, and as a lodge in a garden of cucumbers," that is, she will be isolated, visible but alone, in a field of comestibles. In these similes, Isaiah introduces yet another of his major themes, that despite their wickedness and despite the trials that they will face, the people of Israel will survive — or at least a remnant will survive. The country may be devoured, like the grapes in the vineyard or the cucumbers, but the daughter of Sion, like the covert and the lodge, will survive. Furthermore, the daughter of Sion will also be like "a city that is laid waste," which seems to clash with the similes of the covert and the lodge. But his third simile returns us to verse 7, "Your land is desolate, your cities are burnt with fire," and reminds the audience that while the daughter of Sion will survive, it will be at great expense, both of individuals and of the society as a whole.

In these five verses, then, Isaiah, by yoking together so many seemingly disparate similes and metaphors, has not only warned the people but has also introduced a number of the themes that will run through the book; and the abrupt shifts, along with the vehemence of the speech, forces the audience to be aware of the wider implications of the prophet's message, so that he can then proceed to his famous condemnation of empty ritual, culminating in the advice, "Learn to do well." In addition, in these few verses the prophet has used six different images for Israel, images that ordinarily have no other relationship to each other. And the metaphoric "daughter of Sion" is itself the subject of the series of similes involving the covert, the lodge, and the city. In order to convey the reality of Israel's situation, the prophet operates simultaneously on a number of imagistic levels.

If the people do indeed learn to do well, what will be the result?

> 18. And then come, and accuse me, saith the Lord: if your sins be as scarlet, they shall be made white as snow: and if they be red as crimson, they shall be white as wool. 19. If you be willing, and will hearken to me, you shall eat the good things of the land. 20. But if you will not, and will provoke me to wrath: the sword shall devour you because the mouth of the Lord hath spoken it.

Here, and throughout the prophets, key themes and images appear in a kaleido-scopic way. The reward for repentance will be dialogue with God and purification. And since the people have just been told "Your hands are full of blood. Wash yourselves, be clean . . ." (15-16), the purification consists, imagistically, of turning the redness of their sins to white. The next verse promises that, if the people repent, they will "eat the good things of the land," which recalls the earlier description of the land as desolate and then as a place devoured by strangers, an image which is picked up again in verse 20, where the prophet's (and God's) anger shows again, contrasting the healthy eating of Israel with the devouring done by strangers.[4]

Verse 21 continues and expands the pattern we have seen developing: "How is the faithful city, that was full of judgment, become a harlot? justice dwelt in it, but now murderers." In an image that the prophets use frequently (e.g., Jeremiah 2:2; Ezekiel 16; and most famous of all, Hosea 1) Israel, here represented by Jerusalem, is depicted as a harlot or an unfaithful wife, an image that refers back to verse 3, "they have forsaken the Lord."

Then, in an abrupt shift, the city that has become a harlot is said to be inhabited by murderers, which may recall the sword of verse 20 and surely recalls the blood-covered hands of verse 15. Thus, what appears at first as a mixed — or at least confused — metaphor in verse 21 actually combines in a new way elements that have already been used, sharpening both the prophet's condemnation and his picture of the ideal relationship between God and Israel. The images do not have to make perfect logical sense in order to be effective. There is no sense here of a strictly logical argument. Isaiah's point is really a simple one: the people have been behaving badly and they need to repent. Each of the images that he uses reinforces this message, revealing new facets either of the people's evil or of the possible good that could exist; and the images recur and are expanded, albeit in no special order, throughout the chapter and the book.

After the metaphor of verse 21, Isaiah becomes more literal in verse 23: "Thy princes are faithless, companions of thieves: they love bribes, they run after rewards. They judge not the fatherless: and the widow's cause cometh not in to them." Ordinarily this verse might have followed verse 17, "Learn to do well: seek judgment, relieve the oppressed, judge for the fatherless, defend the widow," for it indicates exactly how the leaders do not "do well," but the intervening five verses, with their promise of forgiveness and their metaphoric picture of what Israel has become, make verse 23 more striking and more effective. It is not simply that the leaders have money and ignore justice or that they favor the strong over the weak. These are only examples of a greater evil, that the leaders — and all of Israel — have been unfaithful to God. The multitude of sins is symptomatic of the problem as Isaiah expressed it in verse 3: "The ox knoweth his owner, and the ass his master's crib: Israel hath not known me, and my people hath not understood." The ox and even the ass know

to whom they owe their well being; but Israel, which stands in the relationship
of a beloved child or wife to God, does not understand. Thus the prophet's task
is to teach the people and to move them, so that they will both understand and
do what they should, and he approaches that task through poetic prophecy,
providing, as I hope to show, a model followed by Langland over two thousand
years later.

The first chapter of Isaiah closes with the promise, both hopeful and terrible,
that if the people do not repent, God will purge them, another of Isaiah's favorite
images, and then will reestablish the nation in justice: "After this thou shalt be
called the city of the just, a faithful city" (verse 26). When justice is reestablished, when the people have learned to do well, the city, which has been a
harlot, will be faithful once again. This promise, which might be called
apocalyptic, is based on the imagery that has informed the whole chapter and
seems like a fitting conclusion to the opening prophecy; but there are still five
verses left, verses that describe briefly the "faithful city" but that then return to
the theme that between now and then there will be hard times: "30. When you
shall be as an oak with the leaves falling off, and as a garden without water. 31.
And your strength shall be as the ashes of tow, and your work as a spark: and
both shall burn together, and there shall be none to quench it." If the people
repent, conditions will improve. If they do not repent, conditions will
deteriorate and then improve. Clearly the first way is preferable, but Isaiah
knows that the people are not likely to repent, and he therefore concludes his
chapter not with a consoling picture of the city restored but with an image of the
destruction that will necessarily precede the restoration. His object here is not
to console. It is to disturb, and so he concludes with a chilling picture.[5]

This first chapter of Isaiah is typical of many chapters in the prophets,
chapters that are full of various images that seem either to be unconnected or
to clash with each other but that in fact complement each other, building up an
emotional picture that the prophets hope will stir the people to repentance. This
is not, however, the only method by which the prophets communicate their
messages. There are many examples throughout the prophets of individual
images developed at great length. This is true of a number of chapters in Ezekiel
(e.g., chapter 16 on Jerusalem's unfaithfulness; chapter 23 on Oolla and Ooliba;
or chapter 37, which combines the vision of dry bones and the image of the joined
sticks) and Jeremiah (e.g., chapter 13 on Jeremiah's girdle or chapter 27 on the
chains that Jeremiah sends), as well as in Isaiah. One striking example is Isaiah
5, the Song of the Vineyard, which describes in detail the planting of a vineyard
and the planter's disappointment that the vineyard has brought forth only wild
grapes, followed by Isaiah's exposition of the transparent allegory: "for the
vineyard of the Lord of hosts is the house of Israel: and the man of Juda his
pleasant plant: and I looked that he should do judgment, and behold iniquity:
and do justice, and behold a cry" (5:7). This short allegory is clear and effective,
but it does not end with Isaiah's exposition, for Isaiah continues to describe what

will happen to the vineyard, then shifts to consider the people's drunkenness ("Woe to you that rise up early in the morning to follow drunkenness ..." 5:11) and the people's unwillingness to regard their proper labor ("The harp, and the lyre, and the timbrel, and the pipe, and wine are in your feasts: and the work of the Lord you regard not, nor do you consider the works of his hands" 5:12), and he adds that part of the appropriate punishment consists of thirst. Much of Isaiah 5, then, is based on the symbol of the vineyard, which is drawn out to illustrate God's disappointment in his people, their sins, and the nature of their punishment.

Chapter 5 is not the end of the vineyard, however. In Isaiah 27 we read, "1. In that day, the Lord with his hard, and great, and strong sword shall visit Leviathan the bar serpent, and Leviathan the crooked serpent, and shall slay the whale that is in the sea. 2. In that day there shall be singing to the vineyard of pure wine. 3. I am the Lord that keep it, I will suddenly give it drink: lest any hurt come to it, I keep it night and day." Here, after twenty-two chapters (which may have nothing to do with the order of composition), the vineyard reappears with its original allegorical meaning intact. And after another thirty-eight chapters, it appears again: "And they shall build houses, and inhabit them; and they shall plant vineyards, and eat the fruits of them" (65:21). Although in this instance the vineyard will be planted by the people and will flourish, these vineyards are analogous to the ones mentioned earlier: the people's vineyards will flourish because the people themselves, God's vineyard, will flourish.

Furthermore, like many other such images, the image of the vineyard recurs in the other prophets. Jeremiah, for example, says, "I planted thee a chosen vineyard, all true seed: how then art thou turned unto me into that which is good for nothing, O strange vineyard?" (2:21), and Ezekiel creates an extended allegory about a vineyard (17:1-10). Vineyards play similar roles in a number of the Minor Prophets and are, of course, used extensively in the New Testament as well. To a medieval reader, the recurrence of such images would be seen not as a coincidence, of course, nor even as evidence of social conditions or literary influence. Rather it would indicate the essential unity of the works in which the images appeared and reinforce the validity of their messages. We can see such tendencies in Jerome's commentaries, for instance, in which he illustrates his interpretation of a word or phrase by quoting every verse he can recall in which the word or phrase appears. In such lists, chronology is unimportant, for the whole Bible speaks with one voice, that of God, and time disappears.

The Song of the Vineyard illustrates yet another technique of the prophets, their tendency to use allegory in presenting their messages. It is common, when speaking of the study of the Bible in the Middle Ages, to talk in terms of allegory, though typology would be a more appropriate term. Such typological readings, however, are often imposed on the prophets from the outside. The prophetic texts themselves are full of little allegories which, like the image we saw earlier, need not be consistent. These prophetic allegories are almost always transparent, and the prophets frequently elucidate them just to be sure they are understood, as Isaiah does in 5:7, where he explains that the planter of the vineyard is God, the vineyard is Israel, and the pleasant plant is Judah. Such allegories may take several verses, like the Song of the Vineyard or Ezekiel's vision of dry bones, or they may occupy a single verse, like Isaiah 9:14, "The Lord shall destroy out of Israel the head and the tail, him that bendeth down, and him that holdeth back, on one day," which he then explains in the next verse, "The aged and honorable, he is the head: and the prophet that teacheth him, he is the tail."

Another way in which the prophets caught their contemporaries' — and our — attention is through allegorical actions. Isaiah, for example, in order to show the fate of Egypt and Ethiopia, goes barefoot and naked (20); Ezekiel is commanded to sleep on his left side for three hundred ninety days and on his right side for forty days (4:4-6); and Jeremiah sends chains to a number of kings to indicate their coming enslavement to Babylon (27). While the allegorical import of Jeremiah's act is relatively clear, that of Isaiah's or Ezekiel's is less so and requires the prophets' explanations. Without such explanations, the prophets surely would seem — and may have seemed to their contemporaries — little short of mad; but with those explanations we can see the strength of the prophetic impulse.

The purpose of this brief survey of the prophets has been to indicate some of the ways in which the prophets' use of language can be viewed as poetic, that is, as finely wrought language, in verse, employing carefully thought out structures and images. While detailed analyses of prophetic poetry would be out of place here, they are clearly required for any study of the prophets, for, whatever their divine inspiration may have been, the prophets, and generally their editors as well, were clearly careful literary craftsmen who showed a great deal of care not only for what they said but for how they said it. We may not always be aware of this dimension of prophetic writing, but if we take the time to examine the prophet's words, we can see not only the power of their teaching but also their formidable literary skill.[6] What we must see now is the extent to which our medieval forebears may have recognized this aspect of prophetic activity.

3. THE PROPHETS IN THE MIDDLE AGES

It would indeed be convenient if there existed a comprehensive survey of attitudes toward the prophets throughout history. Such a work, however, does not exist, and what follows will not serve in its place; but, having examined the prophets in their own time and the prophets as literary craftsmen, we must now glance briefly at how the prophets were regarded in later times in order to justify and clarify Langland's use of them as literary prototypes. The remainder of this section will attempt to describe some attitudes toward the prophets before and during the fourteenth century. One caution is in order here: aside from the biblical sources themselves, we have no way of knowing which of the sources that will be cited Langland actually knew. What this section of the argument will establish is that in using the prophets as he did, Langland was being perfectly consistent with medieval ideas about the prophets.

The Babylonian conquest of Judah in 586 B.C. marked a change in ideas about prophecy. Shortly after the conquest, Jeremiah and Ezekiel were both dead; and the prophecies of Deutero- and Trito-Isaiah, written well into the period of exile, were apparently assimiliated at an early date into the prophecies of the earlier Isaiah. Thereafter, as Blenkinsopp notes, following the loss of national independence there was more reference to the earlier prophets: "With the availability of prophetic material in writing, the emphasis was less on direct inspired utterance and more on the inspired interpretation of past prophecy" (256). The preservation of written texts, and the prominent place of those texts in the national consciousness, made them the basis for much future prophecy, both in the late Old Testament and the New Testament periods.

In many ways the New Testament can be seen as a continuation of the prophets. Not only is Christ seen as the fulfillment of Old Testament prophecy, but he even presents himself as a prophet (Matthew 13:57); and, as we have seen, his teachings in relation to the ritual and moral laws is clearly in the tradition of the prophets. Furthermore, Paul and the authors of the other epistles rely heavily on the prophets. This is particularly true of the epistles of James and Peter, which have often been seen as originating in a Hellenistic Jewish context and which emphasize the religious element in proper moral behavior, just as the prophets do. Thus we read in James, "Religion clean and undefiled before God and the Father, is this: to visit the fatherless and the widows in their tribulation: and to keep one's self unspotted from this world" (1:27), a clear reference to Isaiah 1:17, as is also 1 Peter 2:15, "For so is the will of God, that by doing well you may put to silence the ignorance of foolish men." Like Isaiah's "Learn to do well" (*Discite benefacere*), Peter's "That by doing well" (*ut benefacientes*) stresses the importance of right action. Of course the arguments over the relative values in the Bible of faith and works, elements which are so important in *Piers Plowman*, have been going on for centuries; and one of the reasons that they will never be settled is that various parts of the Bible support each side. Those portions that emphasize works tend to sound like the prophets, though in discussing medieval readings we must be careful not to give those passages too Pelagian a reading.

What is important for our purposes, however, is not so much what the Bible itself says as how it has been interpreted, and especially how the prophets have been viewed. A simple view might focus only on the predictive powers of the prophets, reinforced by typological criticism, but such a view would omit some important aspects of the subject. For instance, G. W. H. Lampe notes that in early Christian writers "The interpretation of prophecy seems sometimes to be less a declaration of the fulfillment of God's purposes in Christ than an assimilation of Christian life and worship to Old Testament models. . . . Such a use of prophecy seems arbitrary; but it was considered to be justifiable on the ground that the prophets were actually preachers of the Gospel before the event" (167). The Old Testament was not seen, then, just as a foreshadowing or prediction of the New. Rather, since the prophets were preaching the Gospels before the Gospel events took place, the Old Testament furnished a model, a model that was still applicable both in New Testament times and in the present. It is this continuing relevance of the prophetic texts that most concerns us here. Those texts were not rendered out of date by New Testament history. They were not even seen as slightly outmoded, the way a model might be viewed. They continued to be seen as vital aspects of the Bible, even if this view required the imposition of various kinds of allegory.

Among the early Church Fathers, the emphasis was on the predictive powers of prophecy. Cassiodorus, for example described prophecy as "a divine exhalation which proclaims the outcome of things either through deeds or through words with immutable truth." Both Jerome and Augustine emphasized predictive powers in their overt comments on the prophets. In Jerome's commentary on Isaiah, "There was hardly a page where Jerome did not emphasize that Isaias was perpetually talking about Christ. The first chapter of the book pictures the people of Juda as one grievously wounded. The picture, Jerome said, 'refers to the last captivity, the one that came after Titus and Vespasian', thus the disaster which Jesus had predicted. In the same chapter, the apostrophe 'Are not those hands stained in blood?' is addressed directly to Christ's executioners, who 'have shed the blood of the just'" (Steinmann 309). Thus for Jerome, prophecies are largely Christological,[7] though they may also, like Ezekiel's vision of the rebuilt Temple, refer to developments in spiritual life. For instance, about the eight steps in Ezekiel 40:31, Jerome notes that seven would not be enough. "Here there are eight steps, with which we pass from the synagogue to the Church, from the Old Testament to the New, from earthly to heavenly things" (578). Nevertheless, throughout his commentaries on both the Major and Minor Prophets, Jerome constantly finds contemporary applications of the prophetic words. Often, it is true, these applications consist only of further attacks on the Jews — they are, Jerome says, as bad now as they were when the prophets prophesied — but occasionally he can move beyond this level, especially when he wants to attack contemporary heretics, whom he compares to the false prophets or to those children of incest, the Ammonites. Even more to our point is his use of the prophets to attack corruption in the Church: "Like Aggaeus, Sophonias attacked the priests of Juda. Jerome applied their messages to the Christian priesthood, though he foresaw there would be protests" (Steinmann

207). Here Jerome does not rely on the prophets' predictive powers, as he did in his comments on the Jews, or on allegory, as he did in making the false prophets into types of the heretics. Instead, he sees a contemporary relevance in the prophetic condemnation: those abuses that the prophets attacked continue to exist, which makes the prophetic words still viable in the most literal terms.

Augustine's emphasis on the prophets as foretellers can be seen in his definition of the Age of the Prophets as the time between Samuel and the rebuilding of the Temple, "although, of course, the patriarch Noe ... and others before and after him up to the time of the kings, were Prophets also. At least, they prefigured, in some fashion, many things touching the City of God and the kingdom of heaven, and sometimes actually prophesied" (*City* XVII,1). It is interesting that for Augustine, when visions are involved in prophecy, it need not be the prophet who has the vision. Thus "Joseph, who understood the meaning of the seven ears of corn and the seven kine, was more a prophet than Pharaoh, who saw them in a dream; for Pharaoh saw only a form impressed upon his spirit, whereas Joseph understood through a light given to his mind" (*Literal Meaning* 189). That is, one who has visions is a lesser prophet than one who interprets them; but the highest is one who both has and interprets the visions (*Literal Meaning* 189-90). Of course his example of such a prophet is Daniel, who divined and interpreted the dream of Nebuchadnezzar (a dream that the king refused to divulge, in order to test Daniel's interpretive powers!). Still, Augustine recognized another function of the prophets when he declared that they came "as God saw fit to send them, to predict what needed prediction, or to rebuke vice and teach virtue" (*City* XVII,2).

Gregory in his homilies on Ezekiel shares the idea that prophecy means foretelling. In fact he argues that there are three times with which prophecy is concerned, the past, the present, and the future, but that two of these are etymologically incorrect, since prophecy means foretelling the future, although the Bible itself gives evidence of all three. Gregory's reconciliation of this apparent inconsistency requires him to explain that prophecies about the present disclose hidden things, that, in other words, the prophet can see the cause of the future in the present. As Gregory says, "Let us consider the order of prophecy. From reflection it comes to dream (*somnium*), from dream it reaches to the future. Whoever therefore discovers the root of a dream truly from the past has examined what may be said about the future" (6-7). Gregory not only recognizes that the prophet foretells the future by reading the present, but he also points out the role played by the prophet's inner life as manifested in dreams. After the efforts of Jerome and Augustine to prove that Christianity was the fulfillment of Judaism as the prophets had foretold, Gregory seems to have taken that point for granted, mentioning it often but seeking other significance, more in keeping with the nature of homilies, in his study of Ezekiel. Gregory's exposition tends to have far more universal significance than does that of Jerome, and it makes the prophets more relevant for a contemporary audience.[8]

We can easily find medieval theologians who emphasized the predictive approach. Thus, according to the *Summa theologica* attributed to Alexander of Hales, "the 'preceptive mode' is found in the Pentateuch, the 'historical and exemplifying mode' in the Historiographic Books, the 'exhorting mode' in the Sapiential Books, the 'revelatory mode' in the Prophetic Books, and the 'orative mode' in the Psalter" (Minnis 1984, 65). For Alexander, precepts and exhortation have their focus elsewhere. The dominant mode of the prophets is revelation. This is the sense we get as well from Thomas Aquinas, who says, "The revelation of future events most properly belongs to prophecy" (2. 171,3). Like Gregory, Aquinas uses a mistaken etymology to define the prophet as a foreteller of the future.[9] Aquinas is, in fact, quite distant from the view of the prophets as reformers. He holds that prophecy can relate to "all realities, whether they be human or divine, spiritual or corporeal." Yet, "because prophecy relates to what is far from our range of knowledge, then the more a reality is distant from human knowledge, the more properly will that reality belong to prophecy" (2. 171,3). This position on the prophet contains some serious problems, among them the question of whether a prophet's announcements can be false. If we assume an "if" clause in the prophets and see the prophet's emphasis on repentance, then even a Jonah, whose predictions did not come true, cannot be said to have been false or mistaken. But without that "if" clause, it would appear that all the prophets made mistakes. Aquinas deals with such "mistakes" by explaining that Divine foreknowledge sees future events in two ways, in themselves and in their cause. This double knowledge exists for God but not for the prophets. At times, "prophetic revelation only reproduces from divine foreknowledge a knowledge of the relations of cause to effect. Events in that case can come to pass in a way other than they have been foretold." Thus real prophecy may not come true, but it is not subject to error (2. 171,6). Certainly this is an interesting and important philosophical approach to the problem, but it is far removed from what the prophets intended, the indication and correction of error. The only importance of the prophets according to this account lies in their predictive powers.

The other approach to the prophets, looking at them for what they tell us about the proper conduct of our lives, in consonance, of course, with the New Testament, also appeared at various times in the Middle Ages, particularly in the interest of reform. Peter Damian, for example, "incessantly appealed in the cause of the reform both of monasticism and of the whole Church to arguments drawn from the Bible, and especially from the Prophets" (Leclercq 188). St. Bridget of Sweden, herself revered as a prophet, often behaved like one: she "constantly intervened in the public life of the age in which she lived, and with an astonishing perspicacity as well as an indomitable courage she rebuked immorality and godlessness wherever she found them" (Lindblom 25). For such people, the correct response to "immorality and godlessness," to corruption that appeared in the Church or elsewhere in the society, was the response of the prophets: exhortation to right action. Their point was, as Isaiah had said, "Cease to do perversely. Learn to do well."

One of the most interesting discussions of prophecy is found in MS. Douai 434, Question 481, which, according to Jean-Pierre Torrell, was written by Hugh of St.-Cher.[10] In this work Hugh refines some ideas about prophecy. For example, he indicates that not everyone who has a revelation is a prophet. A prophetic revelation, according to Hugh, cannot come from either an angel or a demon; it must come from the Holy Spirit. Nor is everyone who sees the future a prophet: in John 11:50, Caiaphas appears to tell the future, but he is not a prophet because he lacks the proper intention, so that while the act that he predicted was inspired by the Holy Spirit, Caiaphas' intention was not so inspired and consequently he cannot be called a prophet (46-47). In fact, Hugh denies that a prediction that must come true is a prophecy. True prophecy, therefore, deals with a future that is contingent, a future that relies, as we saw in the prophets themselves, on the "if" clause. Thus when Jesus tells Peter, "Ter me negabis" (Matthew 26:34), he is not prophesying but predicting the future (43).

Hugh does, however, deal with the methods of prophecy. As Torrell explains, Hugh tries to describe the prophet's role in transmitting the word of God: "To what extent is man an adequate instrument in the hands of the divine? The word that he announces is not intended only for his contemporaries but also for generations to come; originating from higher than himself, it also goes much further. How can he not be a deficient instrument?" (263). In this way Hugh acknowledges both the specialness of the prophet as well as his humanness: the prophet is chosen, but he is still human.

While Hugh has many important things to say about prophecy, some of them are more pertinent than others to our study of *Piers Plowman*. Among these are Hugh's analysis of the stages of prophecy, his description of two *specula* that the prophet uses, and his description of the role of imagination in prophecy. Although we have no way of proving that Langland had read such medieval works on prophecy, his attention to these matters must argue for some familiarity with such works.

For example, Hugh describes three types of prophetic acts, which also constitute three stages of prophecy: the apparition of the image (*ymaginum*) by the imagination (*vis ymaginativa*), the revelation of what lies beneath the image, and the announcement (*denonciatio*) of the revealed reality (10-11). There are several points here that require consideration. One is that each of these types of prophecy is illustrated by a biblical example. The lowest type is represented by Pharaoh, who simply had a prophetic vision, according to which he can be called a prophet. The second type is represented by Joseph, who both had and revealed the meaning of prophetic visions (as he also revealed the meaning of

Pharaoh's visions). And finally the highest type, that of prophecy which receives the visions, reveals their meanings, and announces them, is represented by Daniel, Isaiah, and Jeremiah (11). Thus, to jump ahead again, in *Piers Plowman* we see Will receive the visions, we see him (or other characters, some of which represent his internal faculties) explicate those visions,[11] and we see him announce those visions in the work that we call *Piers Plowman*. In connection with this last point, it is interesting to consider Hugh's use of the word (*denonciatio*), which means both "announcement" and "denunciation." As we have seen, both meanings of the term are appropriate for the prophets, whose "announcements" are frequently denunciations. Here we might think of Abelard's comment in the prologue to his "Commentary on Romans," that "the prophetical or historical books together with the other Scriptures, exhort us to act upon the precepts which have been given and stir men's affections to obey those precepts" (Minnis 1988, 100). To put it briefly, the point of the prophetic *denonciatio* was to make people do well.

What Hugh says about the *vis ymaginativa* is also important. Bloomfield (1961, 170-74) discusses the importance of Ymagenatif for Langland and identifies a possible source for Langland's use of this character in such Arab philosophers as Al-Farabi and in Maimonides, who associated imagination and prophecy. Recently Kaulbach has explored the relationship between Langland's Ymagenatif and Avicenna's association of imagination and prophecy in a manuscript in the Worcester Cathedral Library that might have been available to Langland. According to Kaulbach, "The '*vis imaginativa secundum Avicennam*' transforms the prophet's abstract moral intuitions into images which impel the prophet to both speak and write down such convincing words that his imagination reforms him and his society" (498-99), which is a good description of what happens in Langland's poem.

A final point about these types or stages of prophecy is that they move from passivity to an increased level of activity. The reception of images is essentially a passive act, while the latter two types require more action. Here again we find a correspondence in *Piers Plowman*, in which Will begins by receiving his visions, then becomes more of a participant in them as he seeks to clarify the meaning of what he has seen, and finally "announces" those visions in his prophetic poem.

Yet another aspect of Hugh's discussion that is relevant for Langland is Hugh's description of the two *specula* by means of which the prophet has his visions, an aspect of prophecy discussed also by Philip the Chancellor and Alexander of Hales, among others. For Hugh, "the prophetic vision requires the mediation of a created intelligible idea, thanks to which the prophet sees the reality" (Torrell 129; 27). As Torrell explains the concept, for Hugh there are actually two mirrors. One is the *speculum creatricis essencie*, which is eternal and through which the Creator can be apprehended. The other is the mirror of creation (*speculum creature*). Torrell says, partially paraphrasing Hugh, that this is what Paul refers to when he says, "We see now through a glass in a dark manner (*per speculum in enigmate*;" I Corinthians 13:12). "Knowledge *per speculum creature* is the lot of the earth, of our condition as travellers; through this vision ... the creative essence is 'seen' in the mirror of creation by means of the power of reasoning (*per modum ratiocinationis*)" (191). Again, without arguing that Langland knew Hugh specifically, he could have been acquainted with the terms that Hugh — and Alexander and Philip — used in discussing prophecy, as we can see in his use of the "myrrour þat hihte Myddelerd" (XI. 171), through which Will sees the objects and the events of the rest of Passus XI and all of XII and XIII. That mirror reflects the world as it really exists, characterized by Recklessness, whose views are so often mistaken. In this mirror Will first sees the human world, then the natural world, and he awakens in XIII because of his questioning of Reason (recalling, perhaps, Hugh's *ratiocinatio*), that is, because of his concern with metaphysical speculation rather than with the concrete lessons he has been shown. Just as the prophets were concerned more with concrete points than they were with metaphysics, so Will has to learn what to do and not be so interested in metaphysical speculation that can distract him from doing well. It is significant, then, that at this point he meets Ymagenatif, who also has prophetic overtones. It should be clear that whatever Langland's sources may have been, the discussions of the medieval theologians on the subject of prophecy contributed to *Piers Plowman*.

As even this very brief survey has indicated, prophecy was treated in a number of different ways in the Middle Ages. There is one more aspect that we must consider, related again to the predictive powers of prophecy. The focus on these powers is in large part a product of figural or typological interpretations of the Bible, the best discussion of which is still that of Erich Auerbach. As Auerbach says, "Those passages in Paul's Epistles which contain figural interpretations ... are [nearly all] intended to strip the Old Testament of its normative character and show that it is merely a shadow of things to come" (1973, 50). Such figural interpretations, as we saw in Jerome, "changed the Old Testament from a book of laws and a history of the people of Israel into a series of figures of Christ and the Redemption" (1973, 52). Consequently, for many readers the major — if not the only — value of the Old Testament lay in its foreshadowing of Christianity; and if the whole of the Old Testament looks forward in this way, how much more do those Old Testament books written by the prophets, especially in light of the etymology that saw "prophet" meaning "foreteller"!

This approach to the Old Testament began to change in the later Middle Ages. As Beryl Smalley has demonstrated, there was a heightened awareness of the literal meaning of the biblical text, an interest that involved contact between Victorine scholars and rabbis, that led to increased study of Hebrew and a greater interest in the Old Testament. Alastair J. Minnis has followed the implications of these developments into the fourteenth century with some fascinating results for our understanding of how the late Middle Ages read the Bible. Thus, as Minnis points out, there was some similarity in the way that the classical pagan writers and the authors of the Old Testament were regarded, partially because both groups antedated the time of Christ and were therefore thought of as limited in their understanding. "Old Testament writers had a greater degree of *auctoritas* than pagan writers, but these two classes of writers were, as it were, close together on the scale of authorities" (Minnis 1984, 115). Although this treatment seems to slight the Old Testament, it actually worked to further Old Testament study. "Even in the fourteenth century, commentaries on the Evangelists remained quite conservative, relying heavily on received interpretations derived mainly from the Fathers and Saints. Hence, it is no accident that most of the major discussions of human literary activity [that Minnis has just examined] appear in analyses of Old Testament books" (Minnis 1984, 116). Their status on the scale of authorities, above the writings of the pagans but lower than the writings in the New Testament, led to more adventurous commentaries, based on more literal readings of the Old Testament books.

This development leads us to the problem we considered earlier of the literary status of biblical texts. Despite the problems involved in treating them as literature — and despite Jerome's attempts to separate them from the realm of literature — even as early as the twelfth century, "certain scholars — notably Peter Abelard and Peter of Poitiers — had in their Bible commentaries applied to sacred literature the conventions and categories of secular literary theory" (Minnis 1981, 58). From the beginning, and with the increased interest in the literal level of the Bible, the literary study of the Bible grew rapidly. In the thirteenth century, "the fact of the divine inspiration of Scripture no longer interfered with thorough examination of the literary issues involved. The roles played by the human *auctores*, and the literary forms and devices which they had employed in their works, were established as features of the literal sense, as facets of their personal purposes in writing" (Minnis 1984, 74). The approach of Nicholas of Lyra is particularly instructive here, for Nicholas not only was a perceptive critic himself, but he had studied Hebrew and was therefore familiar not only with the Hebrew text of the Bible but with the commentaries of Rashi (see Hailpern). In the prologue to his Psalter commentary, Nicholas was concerned "with the 'mind of the prophet' (*mens prophetae*), the inspired mind of David. Whereas twelfth-century commentators had devoted much space to the 'kind of prophecy' (*genus prophecie*) which God had granted to David, Lyra believed that the prophet had a mind of his own: when God uses human beings as instruments, He must make use of the mental equipment which men actually have. Divine inspiration works on and through the human *mens*" (Minnis 1984, 91). In addition to reminding us that, largely because of the alleged foreshadowings of Christ in the Psalter, David was considered a prophet in the Middle Ages, this passage is of profound importance in my argument that Langland saw himself writing in the prophetic tradition, for it provides a theoretical base that justifies Langland's choice. He does not, like the mystics, have to enter a trance or be possessed in order to deliver a prophetic message. Rather, Divine inspiration, operating through his human *mens*, shows him the evil in his society and compels him to speak out against it. Nor, in light of Minnis' findings, is it surprising that so thoroughly Christian a poet as Langland should have used an Old Testament model for his work, for the Old Testament had, to a greater extent than the New, been treated in literary terms. This is not, of course, to deny the influence of the New Testament as a model for parts of *Piers Plowman*,[12] but there is a palpable sense of the Old Testament in the poem,[13] which we can understand even better when we consider comments like the following from the Prologue to Isaiah in the Wyclif Bible, based on Jerome's prologue: "Not more he is to be seyd a profete, than euaungelist. So forsothe alle the mysteries of Crist and the chirche to cleer ... he pursuede, that not hym thou weene of thyng to come to profecien, but of the thingis passid storie to weue" (III.224). If the New Testament is contained in the Old, as the Wyclif Bible implies here and in the prologue to Psalms, or as Peter the Lombard says in his commentary on Psalms,[14] then Langland's reliance on the Old is perfectly acceptable.

Finally, it is not surprising that Langland cast his fourteenth-century prophetic work in poetic form, for there was at least a semi-tradition of poetic prophecy in English, beginning even with Caedmon. Despite the relative rarity of such prophetic works in the late Middle Ages in England, there were numerous works that proclaimed themselves as prophetic, though these generally mean prophetic in the predictive sense. The most famous of them, perhaps, is the Prophecy of Thomas of Erceldoune, which Stephen Barney has recently called "The most like *Piers*" (1988, 129). In addition, a number of works in the alliterative tradition, works that either influenced or were influenced by *Piers*, are prophetic in the same sense as *Piers*. As Barney says, "From Jeremiah to *Wynnere and Wastoure* is a long way, but clearly the two works form part of a tradition which the Bible continued to influence directly through the centuries" (1988, 130). And we might also consider Boccaccio's clear statement in his "Short Treatise in Praise of Dante" that "poetry is theology" (Minnis 1988, 494). And there was at least one well-known poetic work, contemporary with *Piers Plowman*, that openly declared its own prophetic status, John Gower's *Vox clamantis*.

If Langland can be accused of a certain presumption for casting himself in the role of a prophet, how much more applicable would such an accusation be against Gower, who, in his very title, associates himself with Isaiah and with John the Baptist. In fact, it seems likely that Gower took a large part of his inspiration from Langland, for the *Vox* began as a kind of prophetic condemnation of corruption in the English estates, to which Gower added, after 1381, his attack on the Peasants' Rebellion. In an ironic comment on *Piers Plowman*, which was thought to have encouraged the rebellion, Gower says, "One man helped in what another man did, and another agreed that they would be bad, worse, and worst" (74). Gower also goes on to discuss explicitly many of the aspects of his prophetic work that are implicit in *Piers*, such as the nature of his prophetic dream vision. The point to be emphasized here is that Langland's adoption of the prophetic mode is in no way anomalous, that it was not only recognized but imitated. This is not, however, to overlook the profound differences between Gower and Langland. Gower is, in a sense, play-acting at being like a prophet. He certainly feels strongly about what he is saying, and he uses the prophetic persona to help him say it, but he does not become a prophet. Perhaps one explanation for the differences between Gower and Langland is that Gower's fears for society were engendered by his fears for himself and his social class, whereas Langland's concern was less self-interested. Gower spoke for his class, as Coleman points out (1981b, 129), whereas Langland, in a very real sense, at least tried to speak for God, which may be what Coleman means when she says that Gower's solution to the problem of social divisiveness was "moral and political rather than religious" (1981b, 135). Langland's solutions to the problems he discusses are religious in the prophetic sense, which means that they include the moral and political. Gower was trying to restore the world as he had known it and as he thought it should be. Langland was trying to restore the world as God wanted it to be.

Another medieval prophetic poet was Dante, whose work Guido da Pisa compares to Daniel and Ezekiel (Minnis 1988, 469-70). But a brief look at Dante will help to illustrate Langland's uniqueness. Bloomfield has accurately described the differences between Dante and Langland: "Langland is fundamentally involved in the search for Christian perfection; Dante gives us the Christian truth, the next world, against which our present world must be measured. Langland is oriented towards the transformations of this world. . . . Christian perfection is Dante's theme; the quest for Christian perfection is Langland's" (1961, 173). Dante considers the problems of this world from the perspective of another world. Langland keeps that world in mind, but his view is always on this one. Both authors adopt prophetic stances, but in a sense Langland's version of that stance is more indebted to the Old Testament, Dante's to the New. It should be noted, however, that Dante was not working in isolation, that he represents a step in "that gradual process of literary assimilation by which sacred and secular literature had, in the eyes of its readers, come together in respect of subject-matter, stylistic form, and end" (Minnis 1988, 387). And it is also worth recalling Dante's description of the *Comedy* in his Epistle to Can Grande: "The branch of philosophy to which the work is subject, in the whole as in the part, is that of morals or ethics; inasmuch as the whole as well as the part was conceived, not for speculation, but with a practical object" (Minnis 1988, 462). In this passage, Dante is very close to Langland; and Dante's poem is certainly prophetic. As Natalino Sapegno says, "Dante feels himself invested with [his] mission and thus authorized to speak as a prophet and to address other men as a prophet. . . . He elaborates the grandiose concept that his poem must be a warning to all humanity to set it once more on the straight path" (13). But Dante's poem, like so many other prophetic works, and unlike *Piers Plowman*, is prophetic in what it says, not in how it says it. No biblical prophet takes an extended tour of the afterworld and then in a single extended narrative recounts that tour in terza rima. Dante's work is thoroughly informed by the Bible, but he does not "speak Bible" in the same way that Langland does. Other writers from the earliest days of Christianity had tried to convey the prophetic message, but no one else had adapted both their message and their medium. This combination makes Langland unique.

A number of Langland's successors also adopted a prophetic stance, perhaps under the influence of *Piers Plowman*, though they all, like the biblical prophets, shaped that stance to their own personalities. There is, for example, the *Pearl*-poet, about whom Theodore Bogdanos has written: "It is my conviction that the author of *Pearl* places the same demands on his reader as Dante. He too wants his poem read as an analogue to God's Word" (11). In fact the *Pearl*-poet, with his use of Jonah, his critique of human (and especially courtly) behavior in *Sir Gawain and the Green Knight*, and his use of the prophetic dream vision in *Pearl*, is much closer to Langland and shows the early stages of a *Piers Plowman* tradition.

One more comment by Minnis will help to clarify another aspect of *Piers Plowman*, its relationship to preaching: "Late-medieval exegetes had come to regard many a Scriptural *auctor* in the role of preacher; in their eyes, Daniel and his colleagues were preacher-prophets. The *Vox clamantis* represents a further state in the dissemination and development of such theory: therein, a 'modern' writer adopts the stance of the preacher-prophet, likening his moral position and righteous indignation to those of the two 'ancient' preacher-prophets who are his namesakes, St. John the Baptist and St. John the *auctor* of the Apocalypse" (1984, 177). The basis of *Piers Plowman* has often been sought in fourteenth-century sermon literature (see Owst; Salter, 1969), where there is undoubtedly a strong relationship; but it is not enough to stop there. As Muscatine says, *Piers* "is manifestly not a sermon itself, and its depth and variety of 'digressions' can hardly be matched in any known sermon" (90-91). We should recall, however, that the prophets themselves were thought of as preachers. Richard of Basevorn, for example, calls preaching, "the persuasion of many, within a moderate length of time, to meritorious conduct," and he says later that "After creating man, God preached (if we extend the word 'preaching'), saying to Adam (Gen. 2:17) *For in what day soever thou shalt eat of it, thou shalt die the death*. This was the first persuasion of which we read in Scripture. . . . Then he preached frequently through Moses and some Prophets. . . ." (120, 126). Langland himself makes the association in the B-Text when he says, "The prophete precheþ [it] and putte it in þe Sauter" (III.234), thereby identifying David as both preacher and prophet. In the C-Text Langland writes

> Patriarkes and prophetes, precheours of goddes wordes,
> Sauen thorw here sarmon mannes soule fram helle . . .
>   (VII.88-89)

Here patriarchs and prophets, who are often listed together for alliterative reasons, are associated with preachers. We have, then, a context in which to consider the "sermons" in *Piers Plowman* and to account for their "digressiveness." If *Piers* is modelled on the writings of the prophets, it must contain elements that remind us of sermons, for sermons fill a large part of the prophetic texts.[15]

It is now time to consider Langland more closely. What in his environment prompted him to adopt the prophetic mode? How did he adopt — and adapt — it? And finally, and most important, what are the implications of that adoption for our understanding of *Piers Plowman*? These are the questions that will be treated in the next chapter.

III. William Langland and the Motivations of Prophecy

1. THE FOURTEENTH CENTURY

"Ecce quam bonum et quam iucundum,/Habitare fratres in unum—Behold how good and how pleasant it is for brethren to dwell together in unity" — we read in Psalm 133 (132) and in Passus XX of the C-Text, a verse that helped to inspire the conclusion of *Piers Plowman*, in which we see the absolute failure of brothers to dwell together in Unity (a failure that unfortunately continues today). Of course many circumstances have changed over the intervening six centuries, but the basic motive and method of the corruption have remained the same. To someone like Langland, who saw the world in the prophetic terms of the Bible, such corruption was intolerable. To the extent that such corruption continues today, Langland addresses us, and it is interesting to see how critics over the years have reinterpreted the poem to make it more comfortable, have reinterpreted Dowel, for example, so that it means something other than do well. Even E. T. Donaldson has written that "by a strange quirk of fate, *Piers Plowman* was used by the revolutionists in the uprising of 1381, apparently as propaganda for their movement and certainly as part of the code in which they communicated with each other. Assuredly the author, a moderate and a traditionalist, if not a reactionary, could not have approved of this use of his poem and must, indeed, have been considerably embarrassed by his unwitting mesalliance with John Ball" (108). While Langland undoubtedly was embarrassed that his work was associated with a violent uprising, it certainly became so not by a "strange quirk of fate." In addressing the corruption of the court, of the Church, and of society at large, *Piers Plowman* gave articulate and dramatic voice to many of the complaints that lay behind the rebellion; and it is no wonder

41

that the rebels found inspiration in the poem, though, of course, Langland had never urged violence.

Langland's prophetic stance may well have had its source in his view of history. This is most emphatically not to say that Langland was a historian in any sense that we recognize, but that he operated with a biblical sense of history. We must remember that in the Bible the prophetic books follow the historical books, like Samuel, Kings, and Chronicles, books that provide a context for the prophetic teachings; and the book of Daniel shows an intense interest in history. We know now that the historical books were often compiled by followers of the prophetic schools, but to earlier readers the apparent independence of the prophetic and historical works offered further proof of their accuracy. The chaotic conditions of the fourteenth century, coupled with the omnipresent political and ecclesiastical corruption, appeared to many biblically minded people as evidence that the Apocalypse was at hand. These conditions had a different effect on Langland, who saw himself playing much the same role as Isaiah and Jeremiah had played at the time of the collapse of Israel and Judah.

When we recall the history of the late fourteenth century, the resemblance between the two periods does not seem too far-fetched. As Kings and the prophets make clear, Israel and Judah were destroyed because of the widespread corruption of the rulers, the priests, and the people. It is not necessary to recount here the history of fourteenth-century England except to point out that the rulers, priests, and people were still justifiably seen as culpable. Furthermore, successive waves of the plague were interpreted as God's punishment for the abandonment of Christian teaching, as were various other natural disasters like the famines and the great windstorm that are mentioned in *Piers Plowman*.

There were other parallels as well, perhaps the most striking involving Edward III. To a moralistically inclined observer, the kings of England had not been a particularly distinguished lot. Edward II had been notoriously corrupt, and the events that led to his death and the accession of Edward III were especially odious, involving, as they did, adultery, regicide, and an assortment of other transgressions. By the time of the first version of *Piers Plowman*, Edward III had been on the throne for over thirty years and the promise of his early years had been overshadowed by plagues, famines, corruption at court, and the war with France. Certainly a biblically-minded person like Langland could have seen in this history a repetition of the history described in Fourth Kings, including the succession of kings who "did evil in the sight of the Lord," culminating in the fifty-five year reign of Manasses, who, according to legend, was responsible for the death of Isaiah. By the time of the B- and C-Texts, such a view would have received confirmation in the fifty-year reign of Edward III and in the events of the last years of that reign, with Edward in his dotage, the death of the Black Prince, and the activities of John of Gaunt. Even Richard II, who might have been seen as a modern Josias, turned out to be a failure, another in the succession of bad kings. As Donaldson says, "If we accept the premise that B was writing at the time of the coronation of Richard II, then several of C's alterations become easier to understand. The C-revision was accomplished probably during the eighties, when any optimism that may have been generally felt at the time of Richard's accession would have had time to dissipate in the disorder of the Peasants' Revolt . . ." (119).

If Richard proved to be a disappointment by not being the reformer that Josias had been, it must be remembered that there were many things that needed reforming; and many of them reflected the same kinds of problems that we saw discussed in the prophets. For example, the prophets pointed out the relationship among the religious, political, and moral realms, indicating that the failures in all three were interrelated. Such was the case in fourteenth-century England. Pantin contrasts the gulf that existed between the Church and the king in fourteenth-century France with the close relationship that existed between the two estates in England, where so many of the king's servants were also churchmen (44-45). The mingling of these realms can also be seen in the willingness of Edward "to sell out to the popes if the latter made it worth his while. They usually did, by consulting his wishes before making all important appointments and by regularly granting a proportion of all reserved benefices to his servants" (McFarlane 52). Such close connections between the political and religious realms led naturally to a greater ease of corruption, since there was no one in a position of power who would keep track of others in positions of power except for selfish reasons. What Leff says about the fourteenth-century Church is particularly appropriate here: "The moral failings with which it was charged — simony, pluralism, immorality, greed, injustice — were common to the whole middle ages and indeed to all ages. The failure of the late medieval church lay not in these but in the absence of a countervailing spirituality" (29-30). This is not to say that there was no opposition to the corruption in the "religio-political complex," but that such opposition had to come from outside of the courtly and ecclesiastical circles. As the Peasants' Revolt and the activities of Wyclif and his followers indicate, the opposition was certainly there.

These two phenomena, the revolt and the influence of Wyclif, were at least partially the results of a development that occurred in the reign of Edward III. As Michael Packe explains, "Edward united the aristocracy for almost all his long life, but the decisive contribution of common men to his and his eldest son's victories gave a new confidence to men of low degree who, ever since William's Normans came, had played only a passive role in England's affairs" (301). In addition, the vast number of deaths from plague in the lower classes had given greater value to individual laborers, a development that the lower classes sought to exploit while the upper classes sought to suppress it. All of this culminated in the Peasants' Revolt, in which John Ball "converted an indigenous and hitherto rather harmless theme of Christian egalitarianism into a politically threatening call for social equality" (Muscatine 17). Although the suppression of the revolt may have quashed this extreme egalitarianism, the relationship between the classes never reverted to its earlier status. While this comparison between the fourteenth century and the times of the prophets may seem oversimplified to us, it certainly would not have seemed so to people who consistently saw the world in terms of biblical patterns, to people who "spoke Bible."

In short, the late fourteenth century in England was, as Muscatine calls it, an "age of crisis caused by economic depression, famine, Black Death, the decay of feudalism and repressive legislation to stop that decay" (16).[1] All of these had biblical parallels, and if they indicated that England was a nation in peril, they certainly recalled to some people's minds the perils that were faced by the kingdom of Judah in the days before its collapse. One response to this peril that is of some importance in studying *Piers Plowman* was the Wycliffite phenomenon.

There has been a great deal of dispute over the nature of the relationship between Wyclif and Langland. In the absence of any new evidence, such speculation is fruitless, and we shall never be able to determine who influenced whom and how much. What we can say, however, is that *Piers Plowman* and the social (as opposed to the strictly theological) writings of Wyclif and his followers represent parallel phenomena, phenomena that reflect similar concerns and viewpoints even though they may have developed independently of each other in an environment that encouraged the growth of such views, and even though they may disagree, as Christine von Nolcken has recently argued.

The study of Wyclif is filled with problems, and one of the major problems is that over the course of his long career, Wyclif was anything but a systematic thinker, a characteristic that has led to numerous attacks on the reformer. Norton-Smith scornfully notes, "In all his barbed and repetitious probings, Wyclif never tells us how in terms of an actual church or in terms of an actual political realm his purified society would voluntarily reorganize itself. His powerful criticism suggests from time to time the eventual solution of Henry VII and Henry VIII but Wyclif himself never outlines how this new church and state could evolve a workable social contract" (6). More charitably, and more to the point, Stacey describes Wyclif's reform program as consisting mostly in disendowment, "handing over temporal possessions and reforming authority to the King and his baronial friends and rehabilitating the Church in the simple, unpretentious garb of the first church. . ." (68). Wyclif, that is, was not a social legislator or planner. In a modern sense, he had no detailed plan for restructuring society; but from an earlier point of view, he certainly did have such a plan. We might think here of I Kings 8, in which the Israelites ask Samuel to give them a king. Samuel is reluctant to comply, because he knows that this demand reflects the people's inability to recognize God as their king, a point that God confirms in saying "For they have not rejected thee, but me, that I should not reign over them." In seeking a return to the "simple, unpretentious garb of the first church," Wyclif's plan was certainly to be found in the book that God had written on the subject, the Bible. Wyclif's devotion to the text of the Bible is well known: "Wyclif was called *Doctor Evangelicus* because of his love for the Bible and his constant reference to it . . ." (Stacey 73).[2] There is nothing extraordinary in this, since religious reformers, unless they choose to write their own scripture, have always based their reforms on what they claim to have found in the Bible, a book which is, after all, at least in theory the basis of Western religious thought.

There is more to Wyclif's reliance on the Bible than this, however. Bloomfield, referring to some pages from Etienne Gilson, argues that the reactions against scholasticism in the fourteenth century led to a kind of anti-intellectualism that included a return to the Bible (1961, 49). Aside from his inclusive use of the opprobrious term "anti-intellectual," Bloomfield is correct, for while scholasticism certainly made a valuable contribution to religious life, it also had the undeniable effect of over-intellectualizing religious faith, translating it from the realm of what one does to the realm of what one thinks about. But even aside from scholasticism, the biblical text had become, over the preceding millennium, encumbered with innumerable glosses and commentaries, which, valuable as they might have been, were also seen as obscuring Scripture itself, thus prompting, from a different perspective, a return to the Bible. "Wyclif's view of the all-sufficiency of Scripture sharply distinguished him from the medieval schoolmen who recognized little if any difference between Scripture and tradition, both of which were for them part of *auctoritas*. This melding of Scripture and tradition Wyclif would not have and he was at pains to separate his purely Biblical theology from the medieval view" (Stacey 80-81). Furthermore, according to Wyclif himself, Scripture had been obscured by various actions of the Church. Whether this view was a cause or a result of Wyclif's opposition to the Papacy, it was clear to Wyclif that "'Goddis lawe' must take preference over the decrees and pronouncements of Mother Church as the competent and proper authority for Christian truth and practice" (Stacey 81).

One consequence of this attitude of Wyclif's was the project of translating the Bible into English, which began in about 1382. The objections to this project — after 1407 it was illegal to make or use a translation of the Bible (Hargreaves 393) — betray establishment fear of what might be found in that book; and in light of establishment behavior, their fear was well founded. Thus Wyclif opened the way "for taking God's law into one's own hands; or more exactly for making his words in scripture the sole criterion of truth with the help of reason, the testimony of the saints and fathers and such later authorities as upheld the apostolic tradition" (Leff 520). Wyclif, that is, did not simply discuss the commentaries, but he led people back to a consideration of the original text. As Beryl Smalley says, "Wyclif was far too medieval to reject the Fathers or to imagine the sacred page wiped clean of its glosses, but he did reject the later traditions of the Church. He looked back to the early days when, as he thought, the Gospel had been rightly understood and followed" (Smalley 1969, 208).[3]

If my argument about *Piers Plowman* as a fourteenth-century adaptation of the biblical prophetic books is correct, then the poem shares with Wycliffite thought the primacy of the biblical text, with the difference that the theologian and reformer Wyclif worked to make the Bible available in English while the poet Langland sought to reconstruct particular aspects of the Bible as they applied to the contemporary situation, an approach that can also be seen in the prologue to the later version of the Wyclif Bible, which places a great deal of emphasis on the Old Testament. For example, in discussing certain Old Testament descriptions, the author makes the point that "Outirly a nedy man and begger shal not be among Goddis peple; but pore men shulen not fayle in the lond, therefore ryche men shulen helpe hem with loue, and helpe hem wilfully in here nede" (I.6). Similarly his comments on II Kings have an undeniable contemporary relevance:

> The prosces of this ij. book ou3te to stire kingis and lordis
> to mersy and ri3tfulnesse, and euere to be war of ydilnesse,
> that brou3te Dauith to auoutrie and othere myscheues, and
> euere to be meeke to God and hise prestis, and sore
> repente of hire mysdeedis, and make amendis to God and
> men, and wilfully for3eue wroongis don to hem, and euere
> be war of pride and extorcouns, leest God take veniaunce
> on al the peple, as he dide on Dauith and his peple, and
> euere to be pacient and mersiful, as Dauith was, to get
> remissioun of synnes bifore don, and to gete pees, and
> prosperite, and heuenly blisse withouten ende."
>
> (I.11)

Likewise the third book of Kings "schulde stire kingis and lordis, to be mersyful and pytouse on her sugetis that trespasen a3ens hem, and in alle thingis eschewe ydilnesse, lecherie, tresoun, ydolatrie, and false counceilouris and unwyse, and euere distroie synne, and take counceil at hooly scripture and trewe prophetis . . ." (I.15).

The prologue's comments on Manasses seem especially pointed: "now Manasses settith idolis opinly in the temple of God, and sterith men gretly to do idolatrie, and cherischen hem that breken opinly Goddis heestis, and punysche hem soore, as hethene men either eretikis, that bisien hem to lerne, kepe, and teche Goddis heestis . . ." (I.33-34). The cure for such evils, according to the prologue, was easily available, for God "sente prophetis to hem, that thei schulden turne a3en to God, and thei nolde heere these profetis" (I.24).

If all of these applications of Old Testament motifs to contemporary England operate by implication, sometimes the references become more pointed, as, for example, when Amos' passage "on thre greete trespasis of Damask and on the iiij" is applied specifically to Oxford: "Loke nowe wher Oxunford is in thre orrible synnes and in the fourthe, on which God restith not til he punsche it" (51). Of course such passages reflect a large amount of personal pique at events that had transpired in Oxford, but they also illustrate the ways in which prophetic passages of the Bible maintained a continuing relevance in the late Middle Ages. Both Wyclif and Langland show, whether independently of each other or not, a fundamental reliance on the Bible as a blueprint for how a society should operate. There is nothing especially new about this method. As we saw earlier, Jerome constantly attacked his contemporaries by comparing them to various sinners who were depicted in the Bible; and this practice continued throughout the Middle Ages. The Wyclif Bible is especially vehement in drawing such parallels, and, significantly, it does so in the vernacular, which made its contemporary application of biblical passages more accessible to more people.[4]

One consequence of this use of the Bible, as we saw, is the accusation of vagueness concerning Wyclif's description of what an ideal Christian state should be. In one sense he does not have to be terribly specific about his blueprints because they are there in the Bible; but in another sense, as we saw in our discussion of the prophets, those biblical blueprints are themselves vague. Langland's approach was similar. Isaiah says, with sufficient vagueness, "Learn to do well." If we only knew what that verse meant, perhaps we could do it. A large part of *Piers Plowman* is devoted to trying to explain that verse in order to clarify God's blueprint. As Leff says about the later Lollards, there was "a moral insistence upon individual responsibility before God. Right living was the sole criterion of righteousness; spiritual probity could only be proved in practice" (577). Such also is the case in *Piers Plowman*, where the emphasis is on doing, rather than thinking or believing, well.

Despite the overall vagueness of Wyclif's plan, some aspects of his program are quite clear, if not in the form of positive statements at least in his criticisms. Although much of his criticism consists of commonplaces, the existence of so great a body of criticism bespeaks a need for it; and there can be no question that the Church as a whole, and the English Church in particular, required reform. We need no evidence of influence between Wyclif and Langland to see that in this area, as in their reliance on the Bible, they shared many of the same concerns, though Langland never went as far as Wyclif in denying the legitimacy of the visible Church. What they had in common was the view that the Church had abandoned its commitment to poverty and had become too attached to material goods (Leff 527-28), thereby corrupting its mission in the world.

Wyclif's solution — reminiscent of Dante's — was to exalt secular power. In his *De officio regis* (1378), Wyclif "asserted the king's supremacy over the priesthood and looked to him to reform the church . . ." (Leff 496). If the visible Church was not the real Church, that real Church could only be manifested in a society that encouraged right living. Such a pattern had ample biblical precedent. We need only remember the prophetic condemnations of corrupt priests and empty ritual, accompanied by exhortations to the kings of Israel and Judah. Perhaps the best example is Moses, the political leader, who exercised firm control over the priests. Such examples fit well into Wyclif's doctrines, about which Leff says, "Negatively, they entailed the denial of ecclesiastical power; positively its supersession by the lay power. The bible was the agent of the first, the king — so far at least as England was concerned — of the second. Taken together, and acted upon, they meant revolution" (538). Langland, too, emphasized the corruption of the Church and the attempts of the secular ruler to set matters right, and he, too relied on the Bible for his inspiration. Even if the issue of influence is unclear, and even if Langland did not know specific works by Wyclif, the similarity of many of Wyclif's and Langland's social views is not difficult to see. Clearly such feelings as Langland and Wyclif expressed were in the air, and the two writers (and their followers) gave voice to sentiments that were shared by many, Wyclif as a schoolman speaking to other schoolmen and Langland as a poet-prophet speaking to the people.

Yet another similarity between Wyclif and Langland can be seen in their attitudes toward the events of 1381. Both were reformers, basing their messages on biblical texts or models; both were concerned with corruption in the Church that infected the society at large, and both spoke out fearlessly about their beliefs. But neither of them desired their reforms to take on the violent coloring of the Peasants' Revolt.[5]

The close relationship between Wyclif and Langland can be seen in a work like "Pierce the Ploughman's Crede," a Wycliffite work obviously indebted to *Piers Plowman*, in which we read:

> Wytnesse on Wycliff þat warned hem wiþ trewþe;
> For he in goodnesse of gost grayþliche hem warned
> To wayven her wik[e]dnesse & werkes of synne.
> Whou sone þis sori men [seweden] his soule,
> And overal lollede him wiþ heretykes werkes!
>
> (528-32)

Here, in a work derived from the prophetic *Piers Plowman*, we find Wyclif depicted as a persecuted prophet. Whatever the details of the actual relationship between Langland and Wyclif, clearly they were in some agreement over the conditions of late fourteenth-century England and in certain basic approaches to describing and changing that condition.

Another major figure of the Middle Ages whose ideas should be mentioned in connection with *Piers Plowman* is the twelfth- and thirteenth-century abbot Joachim of Fiore. However tenuous the relationship may have been between Wyclif and Langland, that between Joachim and Langland is even more so. But Joachim, like Wyclif, indicates that certain kinds of thought existed so that

Langland, as I interpret his poem, did not suddenly invent new ways of regarding the Bible and the world. In fact, if Bloomfield is correct, the connection between Joachim and Langland may not be all that tenuous, for Bloomfield argues that Wyclif was familiar with Joachimite speculation; even if he did not read the Joachite texts, which were available in England, he mentions Joachim several times (1957, 302). If Wyclif knew the abbot's work, it would possibly have been available for Langland as well.

Joachim, understandably, is most often discussed in terms of his apocalypticism. It is important to stress the distinction between this apocalypticism and mysticism, for Joachim "was concerned with the kingdom of God in history and, except indirectly, not with the union of the individual soul with God" (Bloomfield 1957, 261). But even as an apocalyptic thinker Joachim did not simply look to the future. The nature of his apocalyptic thought actually required him to pay close attention to human history, both of the past, as recorded in the Bible, and of the present. Thus in discussing the growing sense of apocalypticism after Joachim, Leff says that "there was a growing tendency to identify the pope with Antichrist and to make the sins of the hierarchy the cause of disasters which would befall the world. These feelings were intensified by the periodic upheavals which occurred during the later Middle Ages: the Black Death of 1348-50 was the signal for a renewed outburst of mass flagellation greater than anything which had gone before. . . ." Leff goes on to mention the effects of the Hundred Years' War, the Peasants' Revolt, the career of Rienzo, and the Great Schism of 1378-1415 (5-6), all of which were interpreted in an apocalyptic sense. Such an interpretation, however, required more than a view of the future, for if the pope is identified with Antichrist, it is necessary to know what the pope has done to merit such an identification; and if the sins of the leaders will bring disaster, some attention must be given to what those sins are. Thus Joachim's look into the future has as one of its bases a good look into the present, which may well remind us of the prophets.

This is not to say, incidentally, that all of Joachim's followers, or that all apocalyptic thinkers, share Joachim's methodology and are concerned with the present; but it does help to establish one particular approach to apocalyptic thought in the Middle Ages that has some affinities with the prophetic methodology and with *Piers Plowman*. It is interesting, then, that one of the great Joachimist scholars, Tondelli, "has stressed the fact that Joachim was an exegete rather than a theologian. . . . Perhaps one might go further and say that in some respects he was a poet rather than a theologian — a poet of the meaning of history" (Reeves 132). Of course we are more likely to think of him as a poet than were his contemporaries, but they would certainly have recognized him as an exegete, for Joachim was careful to explain that his skill in reading the present and in understanding history so that he could look to the future came through his understanding of the Bible. His answer to how he could foretell future events was "not through prophecy nor conjecture nor revelation. But God, who formerly gave the prophets the spirit of prophecy, gave me the spirit of intellect, so that in the spirit of God I could understand every mystery of Holy Scripture, as the holy prophets understood who used to teach in the spirit of God" (Reeves 13).

It is significant, then, that Joachim's two most important works are the *Liber de concordia novi ac veteris testamenti* and the *Expositio in apocalypsim*. The first of these is divided into five books. "Joachim's aim in Books One through Four was . . . to work out the parallels between the Old and New Testaments, according to the generations from Adam to Christ and the generations from Christ to the end of the world" (Daniel xxii). Joachim examined the Bible closely, as an exegete must, and found parallels between the Old and New Testaments (a common exegetical exercise) which he then applied to post-biblical times down to his own age and into the future, a fascinating application of typology. Thus his conception of the pattern of the ages is based on the Old Testament, the earlier part of the Bible, which established the typology of the New Testament and of the subsequent ages until the end of the world. Just as the Wycliffites stressed certain aspects of Old Testament history and applied them to their own time, as we saw in the prologue to the translation of the Bible, so Joachim placed a greater emphasis on the Old Testament than many of his contemporaries did. Book Five of the *Liber de concordia*, in fact, is an exposition of the "spiritual understanding of the Old Testament," to which the first four books serve as an introduction (Daniel xxii-xxiii).

The other work, the *Expositio in apocalypsim*, Joachim said, grew out of the *Liber de concordia*. "Joachim viewed the Apocalypse as the New Testament parallel to the historical and prophetical books of the Old Testament. Its eight parts functioned in the period of Christ in the same way that the historical books had before Christ, although the Apocalypse marked a step beyond the letter of the Old Testament" (Daniel xxiii). It is important to see here the attention that Joachim paid to the literal meaning of the historical and prophetic books of the Old Testament as the basis for his interpretation of history. Joachim's understanding of history grows directly out of an appreciation of Old Testament history. As Daniel puts it, the "*Liber de concordia*, the *Expositio*, and the unfinished *Tractatus super quatuor evangelia* constitute a commentary on the Old and New Testaments which was intended spiritually to show the 'laborious end of things' and that peace which the victors will enjoy" (xxiv).

What is important here for our purpose is to notice Joachim's emphasis on history in both biblical and post-biblical times, an emphasis that had a considerable influence on later writers. Joachim's use of biblical history to clarify the patterns of subsequent history differs even from the contemporary work of Otto of Freising, who traced the history of the "two cities" down to his own time, for Joachim paid much closer attention to the Old Testament.

This use of the Old Testament as a key to the patterns of history, which has a parallel in *Piers Plowman*, may well have been a result of Jewish influence on

Joachim. Joachim was actually attacked by Geoffrey of Auxerre (not surprisingly, a friend of St. Bernard) "on his supposed Jewish origin" (Reeves 14). On the other hand, millennarian movements almost necessarily rely on Old Testament prophecy, and not just the prophecy in the apocalyptic sections of Daniel (see Blenkinsopp 46). Whatever the cause, Joachim understood the prophetic insistence on the interrelations between the individual and society, as he taught that "Society must be made perfect before individuals could be perfected in this world" (Bloomfield 1961, 99). Not only does this doctrine distance him from the ranks of the mystics, but it indicates the important role that a literal understanding of the Old Testament played in even Joachim's highly allegorical scheme.

Again, whether Langland personally knew Joachim's work we will probably never know, but the influence of Joachimite ideas, like the popular spread of certain of Wyclif's teachings, makes the notion of *Piers Plowman* as a conscious imitation and adaptation of biblical prophecy somewhat less startling, though its poetic form makes it nearly unique for its time. Langland, despite the tendency of some critics to see him as one, was not a theologian. He was a poet, sensitive to the needs of his community, sensitive to his intellectual milieu, and sensitive to the nuances of the biblical text to which he was so devoted. If he was prompted by contemporary events and sanctioned by contemporary (and earlier) thinkers to speak out with a prophetic voice, his greatest inspiration still came from the Bible.

2. THE BURDEN OF PROPHECY

Before we examine the implications of this approach to *Piers Plowman*, yet another major problem remains to be considered, the question of Langland's presumption in casting himself in the role of a biblical prophet. We may occasionally be moved to compare someone to a prophet because of a certain forthrightness or a sense of moral imperative, but we would probably be suspicious of someone who tried to impress us as a prophet, claiming to possess divine sanction and even inspiration. Of course the twentieth century would regard such claims differently from the fourteenth century, but this is not to say that Langland regarded his claim lightly. His awareness of the burden that had been thrust upon him leads to an almost excessive humility, a characteristic that, as we still see, has often been mistaken for simplemindedness.

If, as I have argued, Langland was moved by the events of his time, as was Wyclif, perhaps both of them under the influence of Joachim of Fiore, and as a result took a prophetic stance in his poetry, he certainly could have claimed that he was operating in good biblical tradition. For example, in I Corinthians 14, Paul gives the following instructions: "1. Follow after charity, be zealous for spiritual gifts; but rather that you may prophesy. 2. For he that speaketh in a tongue, speaketh not unto men, but unto God: for no man heareth . . . 3. But he that prophesieth, speaketh to man unto edification, and exhortation, and comfort . . . 5. And I would have you all to speak with tongues, but rather to prophesy." One of the consequences of following after charity, surely a significant phrase for *Piers Plowman*, is the ability to prophesy, which, as a means of edifying, exhorting, and comforting, is itself a kind of charity. Furthermore, everyone was entitled to prophesy: "For you may all prophesy one by one; that all may learn, and all may be exhorted" (I Corinthians 14:31). This passage echoes an episode in Numbers, when Eldad and Medad prophesy and Joshua urges Moses to stop them. Moses' response, a sign of his charity and humility, is "O that all the people might prophesy in the camp" (Numbers 11:29). The ability to prophesy is not restricted to him. He wishes that everyone had the ability, and the implication is that everyone can have the ability, that prophesying — being a true prophet — is a matter of inspiration, not a sign of pride. And it is precisely at a time of great corruption, of the greatest need of prophecy that the prophet is, like Will, the most isolated. Although there were schools of prophets in biblical times, the prophets, as we saw, portray themselves as solitary figures operating at God's command. As Amos tells Amasias, "I am not a prophet, nor am I the son of a prophet: but I am a herdsman plucking wild figs. And the Lord took me when I followed the flock, and the Lord said to me: Go, prophesy to my people Israel" (7:14-15). Like Will, who "shope me into shroudes as y a shep were (Prol.2)," Amos was a shepherd turned prophet at a time of need, not necessarily a learned man and certainly not a member of a prophetic band.[6]

In fact Langland paints a similar picture of Will in *Piers Plowman*. Donaldson, in his excellent study of the C-Text, spends a number of pages examining Langland's use of minstrels in all three texts (Donaldson 140-55), but his conclusion is reminiscent of Tristram Shandy's conclusion about noses: "For by the word *Nose*, throughout all this long chapter of noses, and in every other part of my work, where the word *Nose* occurs, — I declare, by that word I mean a Nose, and nothing more, or less" (Sterne 218). Donaldson's conclusion is that when Langland tells about minstrels, he means by that — minstrels. This conclusion, however, is not where Donaldson's argument has been leading. While it is not necessary here to rehearse all of that argument, it should be pointed out that Donaldson is quite correct in noticing Langland's apparent inability to make up his mind about minstrels, as can be seen in the variations among the texts. In the C-Text, more emphatically than in the other two, Langland makes a clear distinction between the majority of minstrels, whom he condemns as worldly timewasters and frauds, such as those who "for here minstracie a mede thei asken" (III, 275), and the relatively few good minstrels whom he calls "God's minstrels" and about whom he says

> Clerkes and knyhtes welcometh kynges munstrals
> And for loue of here lord liþeth hem at festes;
> Muche more me thynketh riche men ouhte
> Haue beggares byfore hem þe whiche ben goddes
>   munstrals,
> As he sayth hymsulf, seynt Ion bereth witnesse:
>   Qui vos spernit me spernit.
> Forthy y rede ȝow ryche, reueles when ȝe maketh
> For to solace ȝoure soules suche munstrals to have:
> The pore for a foul sage sittynge at thy table,
> With a lered man to lere the what oure lord suffrede
> For to saue thy soule from Satan thyn enemye
> And fithele the withoute flaterynge of god Friday þe geste,
> And a blynd man for a bordor or a bedredene womman
> To crye a largesse tofore oure lord, ȝoure good loos to
>   shewe.
>   (VII.97-109)

If, like Donaldson, we understand "minstrel" only in the most literal sense, then we must agree with him that "only one of the three substitutes for minstrels was capable of exercising the professional function" (145); but Langland does not say these are "substitutes for minstrels." He says they are "goddes munstrals." Thus they are not so dissimilar from the minstrels who are described later:

> Ryht so, ȝe ryche, ȝut rather ȝe sholde
> Welcomen and worschipen and with ȝoure goed helpen
> Godes munstrals and his mesagers and his mery bordiours,
> The whiche arn lunatyk loreles and lepares about. . .
>   (IX.134-37)

These "lunatyk loreles," perhaps reminiscent of ecstatics who are described in the Bible, have just been discussed earlier in the same passus:

>   moneyeles þey walke,
> With a good will, witteles, mony wyde contreyes,
> Riht as Peter dede and Poul, saue þat þey preche nat
> Ne none muracles maken — ac many tymes hem happeth
> To profecye of þe peple, pleyinge, as hit were.
>   (IX.110-14)

Such people seem to Will to be God's apostles, and shortly after, he calls them "munstrals of hevene" (IX.127).

It is surely more than a coincidence that the further description of this particular class of beggars sounds very much like the description that Will gives of himself, especially in the autobiographical addition to the C-Text that opens Passus V: they care little for money, they go barefoot and breadless (we might recall that in Isaiah 20:2, the prophet describes himself going barefoot and naked), and they show little respect for rank — such are the minstrels of heaven, and such is Will. We have here what Donaldson calls "the assimilation of poet to minstrel" (151), and it should be clear from Langland's description of "God's minstrels" that such people fill the role that prophets had filled in the biblical records,[7] as opposed to the general run of minstrels, who are like the false prophets to whom the true prophets so often refer.[8] Thus the poor, the learned, and the crippled whom Langland mentions as "goddes munstrals" in VII. 105-107 provide the edification, exhortation, and comfort that Paul spoke of in I Corinthians 14. And Will's identification of himself with these "munstrals of hevene" puts him in the ranks of the prophets. The correct conclusion to Donaldson's discussion of minstrels in *Piers Plowman* can be found in one of his footnotes: "Perhaps the poet really visualized himself as a prophet and his poem as a prophetic writing. Its tone suggests a poet who felt confident that he was speaking according to the will of God — one of God's minstrels" (145).[9] This may explain, as well, the variations on the theme of minstrelsy that Langland played in the three versions of his poem, for clearly he had some difficulty, another sign of the humility that he shared with the prophets, in announcing his role as a prophet. But if the prophets were poets whose task was to edify, exhort, and comfort, with the aid of divine inspiration, then Langland was indeed a fourteenth-century biblical prophet. What, then, we must ask, was the nature of that divine inspiration?

3. "IN A VISION ONCE I SAW"

Aside from Rip van Winkle, there is probably no other literary character who sleeps as much as Will. He sleeps out of doors and in church; he falls back asleep as soon as he awakens. And he dreams the most extraordinary dreams! Bloomfield, as we saw earlier, called him "somnivolent," as he described Will's falling asleep during Mass, but Will is not simply a victim of narcolepsy, nor does he exemplify the sin of sloth.[10] Nor is he, strictly speaking, an heir of the French dream-vision tradition, as has been alleged. Elizabeth Kirk, for instance, finds in such elements as the early dream and the mention of the river and the season a suggestion of French romance (16). Langland was undoubtedly familiar with this tradition, but there is another work that begins with the same elements: "Now it came to pass in the thirtieth year, in the fourth month, on the fifth day of the month, when I was in the midst of the captives by the river Chobar, the heavens were opened, and I saw the vision of God." This is, of course, the first verse of Ezekiel; and it mentions both the time of the year and the river. To us, it seems to omit the reference to a dream, but this omission may not have been apparent to a medieval reader. Ezekiel says that he saw the visions of God, and we must ask how someone saw such visions.

The Bible makes only passing mention of how visions come to human beings. A passage in Numbers illustrates the problem: God, speaking to the rebellious Aaron and Miriam, says, "Hear my words: if there be among you a prophet of the Lord, I will appear to him in a vision, or I will speak to him in a dream. But it is not so with my servant Moses who is most faithful in all my house: For I speak to him mouth to mouth: and plainly, and not by riddles and figures doth he see the Lord" (12:6-8). We could see, as many commentators have done, three possibilities: visions, dreams, and "mouth to mouth" communications, the last applying only to Moses. Or we could see two, if we read the end of verse 6 as a kind of parallelism using apposition, thereby equating a vision and a dream. This latter is not a common way of reading these verses, but there are other passages that could support it. For example, when Abraham is commanded to sacrifice Isaac we read, "God tempted Abraham, and said to him: Abraham, Abraham. And he answered: Here I am." After God's instructions, we are told, "So Abraham rising up in the night (*de nocte consurgens*) saddled his ass . . ." (Genesis 22:1-3). Although we are not explicitly told that Abraham's vision occurred in a dream, the passage certainly implies that this is the case. In contrast, when Abraham pleads for Sodom and Gomorrha, he is clearly having a waking vision. (Will, we should remember, also has waking visions, especially in the C-Text.) Furthermore, both Deuteronomy (13:1-5) and Jeremiah (27:25-8, 32; 29:8) link prophecy with dreams (Blenkinsopp 159). Although the biblical prophets seldom refer to their own dreams and often condemn the dreams of false prophets, those condemnatory passages, coupled with passages like that in Genesis, make a clear connection between dreams and prophecy, a connection reinforced by passages like that after Jeremiah's vision of the restoration of Israel, when he says, "Upon this I was as it were awaked out of a sleep, and I saw, and my sleep was sweet to me" (31:26).

Furthermore, the prophetic books frequently resemble dreams,[11] and one of Lindblom's observations, made in reference to ecstatic visions (although the extent to which the prophets had ecstatic visions is open to debate) could have been written about *Piers Plowman*: There is, in such visions, "something irrational and ineffable, something which transcends normal, everyday experience, opening the doors of the supernatural world as they do. Though what the visionary sees may be described vividly and in detail, there is a looseness and lack of structural connection. Time and space seem not to matter, and scenes change rapidly as in dreams" (129). This use of dream-like reality plays a significant role in *Piers Plowman*; and if we can remember that we are reading a prophetic dream-vision, many of the problems associated with the poem, such as the abrupt shifts in time and space, will no longer be problems.

These biblical associations of dreams and prophecy continued to be influential. They seem to be taken for granted, for example, throughout the twelfth book of St. Augustine's *De genesi ad litteram*. In discussing visions, Augustine says, "I consider all these phenomena similar to dreams. Now dreams are sometimes false and sometimes true, sometimes troubled and sometimes calm; and true dreams are sometimes quite similar to future events or even clear forecasts while at other times they are predictions given with dark meanings and, as it were, in figurative expressions." Furthermore, Augustine adds, "When anyone asks me about the origin of the images of bodies that appear in ecstasy, an experience that happens but rarely to the soul, I, in turn, ask about the origin of the images that appear daily to the soul in sleep . . ." (*Literal Meaning* 204). As we saw earlier, Augustine's examples of prophets in this book are Joseph and Daniel, whose prophetic status was confirmed by their ability to interpret dreams. Pharaoh dreamed, which gave him the gift of tongues; but Joseph interpreted the dreams, which gave him the gift of prophecy. "But the greatest prophet is he who is endowed with both gifts . . ." (*Literal Meaning* 190).

If Augustine assumed a close relationship between dreams and prophecy, the greatest authority on dreams in the Middle Ages, Macrobius, made it quite explicit in the names he gave to different kinds of dreams. There are the *somnium* (a dream "that conceals with strange shapes and veils with ambiguity the true meaning of the information being offered and requires an interpretation for its understanding"), the *visio* (a dream that actually comes true), and the *oraculum* (a dream "in which a parent, or a pious or revered man, or a priest, or even a god clearly reveals what will or will not transpire, and what action to take or to avoid") (90). Such dream classifications are obviously related to — and possibly derived from — the visions and dreams of the prophets. John of Salisbury illustrates this relationship when he discusses Macrobius' dream classification in some detail and then classes together "the vision of Africanus, the Apocalypse of St. John the Apostle, the oracles of Daniel and Ezekiel, the dream of Pharaoh and Joseph" (*Policraticus* 83) in his discussion of the significance of dreams.

As an illustration that the association of dreams and prophecy continued in the late Middle Ages, we find Aquinas saying, "That foreknowledge of the future [which, for Aquinas, was a major aspect of prophecy] which comes in dreams is either from a revelation of spiritual beings or from a bodily cause. . . . These modes of knowledge are more active during sleep than when awake, for the soul of one who is awake is taken up with exterior tangible realities. . . . Yet judgment is better disposed, because reason is more rigorous when awake than when asleep" (2. 172,1). Aquinas, relying on Augustine's distinction between having visions and interpreting them, says that while one's interpretive abilities are sharper when one is awake, the ability to receive visions is greater when one is asleep. Dante seems to agree, when he says, "At the hour near morning when the swallow begins her sad lays, perhaps in memory of her former woes, and when our mind, more a pilgrim from the flesh and less captive to thoughts, is in its visions almost divine, I seemed to see, in a dream, an eagle poised in the sky, with feathers of gold . . ." (*Purgatorio* 9.13.20) This view of the relationship between dreams and prophecy is also evident in the visual tradition, in which biblical figures are often depicted having their visions in what appears to be a sleep-like state, even when sleep is not mentioned in the text. For example, Revelations 1:10 reads, "I was in the spirit on the Lord's day," but in the so-called Cloisters Apocalypse, St. John is clearly in a sleeping position. Similarly, Ezekiel makes no mention of sleep in his opening vision, but in a thirteenth-century French Bible at Baltimore's Walters Art Gallery (MS.W.59), Ezekiel is shown comfortably asleep while above his head are the heads of a man, a lion, an ox, and an eagle.

It should be clear by now that whatever problems Langland's Will might have, narcolepsy is not among them; and if his dreams are related to the dream visions of the French romances, it is only in a most roundabout way. Nor does his tendency to fall asleep at critical times indicate that he is slothful. Excessive sleep may be a sign of sloth, but Will's sleepfulness need not be read *in malo*, as the long list of biblical examples illustrates. David Mills says, "If the dream is from the Dreamer's mind alone, it is unlikely to have any wider value and the Dreamer's role is to create his own dream. If it comes from outside him, however, his role is that of prophet, to receive a divine revelation and communicate it to his fellow-men" (187-88), and he notes that it is often difficult to distinguish between these kinds of dreams, because they can be combined. The argument of this study is that *Piers Plowman* so combines them.

It would also be possible that Langland was influenced by such pagan dream visions as the *Somnium Scipionis*; but for someone as imbued with the biblical traditions as Langland, such an influence would seem almost superfluous. His sleep and his dreams, rather, are part of his prophetic stance; and if we think it inappropriate for him to fall asleep in church, we must remember that his dream is a divine vision and that he had a good example in Isaiah, whose theophany, in his sixth chapter, occurred in the Temple. Reading *Piers Plowman* is, then, as Spearing says, like dreaming (142), but these dreams are not frivolous. They are, in the sense that we examined earlier, prophetic.

IV. The Poet as Prophet

1. IMITATION

It is now time to clarify and support my assertion that Langland wrote in imitation of the prophets. When Janet Coleman summarizes her view of what the poem is about by saying that "*Piers Plowman* is a dream vision whose unifying theme is the quest to know the meaning of what each man owes, to himself, society, and God" (1981a, 41), she points to those themes that Langland has in common with the prophets. Morton Bloomfield, too, near the end of his study of the poem, has written, "One of the major themes of this book, although not spelled out as such, is that Langland is a prophetic poet — a poet who felt himself privileged to reveal to his fellow men a coming renewal of justice and love that would transform society and through it the individual" (173-74). While there are predictive passages in *Piers* (III.477-81; IV.108-30; V.168-71; and VIII.343-54, passages that we will examine later), the poem's emphasis is not on the revelation of coming events, a predictive function, but on the revelation of present sin and danger, a prophetic function. Like the prophets, Langland is an angry writer, a man who sees the sinfulness of his society, who recognizes the danger posed by that sinfulness, and who feels compelled to share that vision. At the same time, again like the prophets, he is motivated by his love for his nation. He takes no joy in castigation — in fact, he suffers in his prophetic role — but he knows that he must deliver his message precisely in order that justice and love may be renewed, in order that society may be reformed and thereby transformed.

The poet's anger is probably most apparent in the B-Text, especially in the Pardon scene when Piers, like Moses breaking the tablets of the Law, tears the Pardon (see Trower 404), indicating not the flaws of the Pardon but the inability of the people to accept it. The C-Text, with its revised Pardon scene and its greater attention to the speaker's autobiography, offers a better amalgamation of prophetic stances. It is almost as if Langland began in A with his prophetic message, wrote B as he developed a prophetic voice, and then wrote C as he developed prophetic artistry, which required him to control both the voice and his anger.

The question of artistry, as we saw in examining the prophets, is a vexing one. Can the prophets, writing under divine inspiration, be said to use artistry? To a theologian, perhaps the answer is no; but to a poet, like Langland, who read the prophets with a poetic eye, the answer is certainly yes. What, then, does it mean to say that Langland wrote in imitation of the biblical prophets? Imitation raises a number of problems. We know, for instance, that Petrarch was trying to imitate the classical epics when he wrote his *Africa*, and yet no one would mistake the *Africa* for a classical epic. Such is the case with anything but the most slavish imitations, works that lack any life of their own. Petrarch, steeped though he was in classical culture, was still a man of the fourteenth century; and as a creative artist rather than a glorified copyist, it would have been nearly impossible for him to have written a work that did not reflect the fourteenth century, however classical he tried to make it. Furthermore, the fourteenth century did not even pretend to the kind of historical objectivity that we claim, as we can see, for example, in the numerous paintings of classical or biblical figures in medieval or Renaissance dress. Great artists convey the style of their time. Thus, Poussin's evocation of antique rural simplicity in *Et in Arcadia Ego* clearly belongs to the seventeenth century, and Delacroix's *Dante and Virgil in Hell* is obviously a nineteenth-century visualization of the medieval *Comedy*. We frequently try to recapture the past, for numerous reasons; but we always recapture it in terms of our own time. The Romantic view of *Hamlet* is largely discredited now, because we feel that it tells us more about the Romantics than it does about *Hamlet*. Many critics, like the author of this study, still try to understand works in the context of their own time, but they — or we — must recognize the artificiality of such efforts, even despite the valuable work of the new historicists. Can we — and should we — transcend our own time, our own cultural biases, enough to truly enter the spirit of another time? When Machiavelli dressed like the ancients in order to read their works, he was expressing an ideal, but he was no more like the ancients than a child who wears shoulder pads to watch a football game is like a football player.

We can even see the problem in translations. In the King James translation, the Song of Songs begins

> 1. The song of songs which is Solomon's.
> 2. Let him kiss me with the kisses of his mouth: for thy love
>   is better than wine.

3. Because of the savor of thy good ointments thy name is as ointment poured forth, therefore do the virgins love thee.

The same passage in the New English Bible reads

1. I will sing the song of all songs to Solomon
2. that he may smother me with kisses. Your love is more fragrant than wine,
3. fragrant is the scent of your perfume, and your name like perfume poured out; for this the maidens love you.

These two translations of the same Hebrew passage show not only different facilities with the Hebrew language, but entirely different approaches to the text itself. They tell us not simply what the Bible says, but how it has been read at different times, and how those different times have expressed their reading. And, it should be stressed, these are not imitations of the Bible but translations.

To say, therefore, that Langland was writing in imitation of the prophets is not by any means to say that *Piers Plowman* is a facsimile or a translation of the prophets. It does say that Langland saw the problems of his own time, and their solutions, reflected in the prophets and that he adopted and adapted what he understood as the prophetic voice and prophetic themes. If Langland's use of the prophets occasionally seems odd to us, it is undoubtedly because we read the prophets very differently from the way a fourteenth-century poet read them. Nonetheless, there are clear parallels between Langland's work and the works of the prophets. What follows is an attempt to indicate further the ways in which Langland used the prophets, both in large scenes and in individual passages, and then a consideration of the implications of Langland's reliance on these prophetic texts. I will begin by discussing some possible direct reflections of the prophets, especially Isaiah, in the poem and then move on to the more important question of Langland's prophetic stance, relying on my earlier discussion of prophetic techniques.

2. THE CALL TO PROPHECY

As we saw earlier, each of the Major Prophets provides a detailed description of his call to prophecy, descriptions that in many ways characterize the individual prophets. The call of Ezekiel, related in the first three chapters of his book, is truly extraordinary, and if we today are inclined to say that it represents Ezekiel's attempt to put into words an ineffable experience, we must remember that that vision gave rise to Jewish and Christian mystical writings and foreshadows the themes and images that occur in the rest of Ezekiel's prophecies. Jeremiah's call, on the other hand, is typical of his prophecies, with its intimate conversation between Jeremiah and God, which foreshadows many other such conversations in the book.

Isaiah's call to prophecy, recorded in his sixth chapter, shares a number of traits with those of the other prophets, but again expresses his individuality. Like Ezekiel, he tells us where the theophany took place; but unlike Ezekiel, who saw his vision by the river in Babylon, Isaiah has his revelation in the Temple in Jerusalem. In addition, Isaiah's vision is not nearly as elaborate as Ezekiel's, although both show a heightened sense of formality, as opposed to Jeremiah's. On the other hand, Isaiah has in common with Jeremiah a brevity and directness that are not part of Ezekiel. What they all have in common, however, and what they share with all of the other prophets, is a sense of isolation and unworthiness. From Moses onward, one sign of a true prophet is an almost overwhelming sense of unworthiness. Moses, in Exodus, offers one reason after another for God to choose someone else; Jeremiah, as we have seen, offers his youth as evidence of his unworthiness. Isaiah, having seen the Lord and His train filling the Temple, cries out, "Woe is me, because I have held my peace; because I am a man of unclean lips, and I dwell in the midst of a people of unclean lips. . . ." Here Isaiah is even more emphatic than either Moses or Jeremiah, for he not only refers to his humility but he actually condemns himself for holding his peace, for remaining quietly and without protest among sinners. As St. Jerome explains the passage, "If he did not dare to praise God, it was because he had unclean lips, and he had unclean lips because he lived in the midst of a sinful people. Thus it must be understood: 'Because I kept silent and did not strongly rebuke the impious King Uzziah, my lips are unclean and I dare not sing the praises of God with angels'. . . . We do not say here that Isaiah deserved this blame but that he, through his humility, considered his lips unclean and himself unworthy to praise God" (88). Isaiah's impurity, then, resulted from his silence in the face of corruption; and his purification by the angel carrying the coal enables him to respond to God's question, "Whom shall I send?" with the recurrent biblical phrase, "Lo, here I am," indicating now his willingness to speak out. Like Jeremiah, whose mouth God touches, or Ezekiel, who eats a scroll, Isaiah has been initiated into prophecy, that is, he has become a person who will speak out to his sinful compatriots.

One curious feature about Isaiah's call is that it comes in his sixth chapter rather than in the first, where it more logically belongs. Modern scholarship may explain this curiosity by citing the piecemeal composition or editing of Isaiah's prophecies; but in earlier time such explanations were not available. Jerome pointedly ignores the anomaly: "Isaiah prophesied about Judah and Jerusalem under four kings, as he indicates at the beginning of his first chapter; that is, under Uzziah, Jotham, Ahaz, and Hezekiah. Uzziah having died, under whom were said all the things we have already explained, his son Jotham became king . . ." (83). This explanation, while certainly accurate, does nothing to explain why Isaiah berates himself for keeping silent after five chapters in which he has expressed outrage at the people's corruption. Nonetheless, this short chapter, the shortest among all the calls to prophecy, remains powerful, in part, at least, because of its position away from the very beginning of the book.

Some two millennia after Isaiah's prophecies, William Langland, inspired by a scriptural outlook, found himself unable to remain silent about the corruption that he saw around him and so began to write, in imitation of the prophets, *Piers Plowman*. His debt to the prophets in the A-Text is clear, but in the B- and C-Texts it becomes progressively clearer. It is difficult, of course, to explain why Langland made the changes he did, even when we can be sure that the changes were his and not a copyist's, but a number of them seem to be the result of an increasing debt to the books of biblical prophecy. This seems to be especially true of one hundred and four lines of Will's autobiography that Langland added to the C-Text.[1]

Here I must digress for a moment about the text itself. Derek Pearsall, in using the Huntington manuscript as the basis for his text, has followed its numbering of the passus, beginning with a prologue. As Lawrence Clopper explains, there are two types of C manuscripts: "Type 1 manuscripts proceed as if there were prologues to the *Visio* and the *Vita*. . . . Type 2 C manuscripts count the first passus in the *Visio* and the *Vita* as if they were *passus primus*" (1988, 248). Whichever scheme we use, however, we can see that the first one hundred four lines of the poem's sixth "chapter" contain a new autobiographical passage that is like Isaiah's call to prophecy, which is also found in the sixth chapter of the prophet's book.

One of the interesting points about the first section of Passus V is that the dreamer is not dreaming. Having just awakened from his first dream, he encounters two of the characters from that dream, Reason and Conscience, who chide him for his apparent lack of productive activity. This alternation between dream and waking visions is further evidence that Langland consciously relied on prophetic literature as a model. As we saw earlier, prophecy is often associated with dreams, but Will's encounter at the beginning of Passus V comes in a waking vision, which also has prophetic precedents. *Piers Plowman* is known for its dream sequences, but its waking visions are equally important. We should recall that Aquinas made an interesting distinction between the two kind of visions: "That foreknowledge of the future which comes in dreams is either from a revelation of spiritual beings or from a bodily cause. . . . These modes of knowledge are more active during sleep than when awake, for the soul of one who is awake is taken up with exterior tangible realities. . . . Yet judgment is better disposed, because reason is more rigorous when awake than when asleep" (2. 172,1). The dream revelation, that is, may show greater perception, while the waking vision may evidence more reasoned judgment. While the biblical prophets never explicitly discuss their own dream experiences, they do describe dreams as sources of revelation (e.g., Jeremiah 23:25-28); but there is nothing odd about Will's having a waking vision. Like the prophets, Will has both waking and sleeping visions. Thus, when Bloomfield calls the Dreamer "somnivolent" because in his penultimate vision he is in church "sleeping through Mass" (1961, 128), or when Bowers speaks of him as being slothful, they overlook the association that Langland makes between his own experience and those of the prophets. What may at first look to us like the Dreamer's inability to stay awake, his sloth, is really evidence of the value of his visions and his words. It is no accident, therefore, that in Passus V, after his waking vision, he introduces his second dream with a visit to church:

> And to þe kyrke y gan go, god to honoure, . . .
> Sy3ing for my synnes, seggyng my *pater-noster*,
> Wepyng and waylyng til y was aslepe.

> (V.105-8)

This change of setting emphasizes the waking nature of the opening of the passus and reminds us of Isaiah, whose call to prophecy occurred as a waking vision in the Temple. If we now automatically think of sleeping in church as a sign of boredom or sloth, we must keep in mind the possibility that a church is an appropriate place to have a prophetic vision and that at the point when he falls asleep, the Dreamer is deeply involved in recognizing his sinfulness and praying for forgiveness.

When Will awakens at the beginning of the passus, we find him living in Cornhill, which, Pearsall notes, "had something of a reputation as a resort of London vagabonds . . ." (97). How Will got to Cornhill from the Malvern Hills we do not know, though there may be the hint of a relationship here with the eighth chapter of Ezekiel, in which the prophet is brought "in the vision of God" to Jerusalem in order that he may see for himself — and prophesy against — the corruption there. Consequently, Will's awakening in Cornhill, a center of corruption, is perfectly consonant with his prophetic intentions. So, too, is his being dressed as a "lollere," an idler, with a possible pun on Lollard, one of Wyclif's followers. Will offers his readers no defense of his way of life. He is apparently a Cornhill idler who is little regarded by his corrupt fellows but who has a waking vision in which he is accosted by Reason and Conscience, a meeting that recalls Aquinas' statement that "reason is more rigorous when awake than asleep." Here again we see a reflection of the prophets, who are so aware of their shortcomings: as Will retells his story, he constantly emphasizes his own unworthiness.

Will's actual "call" comes from Reason, who is, as Pearsall notes, "the whole moral faculty as it participates in God's truth" (88). Reason, too, fits into the prophetic pattern that Langland has established, for if Isaiah actually "saw the Lord sitting upon a throne," Ezekiel saw "the vision of the likeness of the glory of the Lord," that is, a manifestation of God that exists at several removes from the Deity. Will, imitating the prophets but not claiming the kind of revelation the prophets had, therefore meets with Reason, who is, in fact, a more earthly manifestation of the divine.

Reason begins the interview by asking what Will can contribute "þat to the comune nedeth," a phrase of central importance in *Piers Plowman*, and Reason suggests such activities as serving in church, farming, or shoemaking, all of which Will rejects:

> "Sertes," y sayde, "and so me god helpe,
> Y am to wayke to worche with sykel or with sythe ..."
>
> (V.22-23)

This sounds much like Jeremiah's excuse that "I cannot speak, for I am a child," and it is rejected just as quickly, as Reason accuses the Dreamer of being an idler. The Dreamer's revealing response is that when he was young, he went to school "Tyl y wyste witterly what holy writ menede/And what is beste for the body .../And sykerost for þe soule ..." (V.37-9). In short, he has studied and knows what is proper for human behavior, but so far, like many recent graduates, he has not found a "Lyf þat me lykede" (41). He has not been able — or perhaps has not tried — to turn his knowledge into action, having confined himself merely to saying prayers for the dead. But as Reason knows, saying prayers for the dead, however important, is not enough. It is not, for instance, among the activities that Reason cited "þat to þe comune nedeth." When Reason quotes from Matthew, "Reddet unicuique iuxta opera eius" ("He will render to every man according to his works", Matthew 16:27), clearly Reason condemns the kind of life that Will has been leading, a life lacking in works.

Reason's condemnation is confirmed by Will's unconscious self-condemnation, for although Will asserts that according to Leviticus

> Clerkes ycrouned, of kynde understondynge,
> Sholde nother swynke ne swete ...
>
> (V.56-57)

apparently referring to the laws regarding priests in Leviticus 21, nowhere does Leviticus forbid the priests to do manual work. What Leviticus 21 does proclaim is that priests should not be so involved with matters relating to death. As Will proceeds with his response, his direction continues to be mistaken: priests, he saw, should "synge masses or sitten and wryten,/Redon and resceyuen þat resoun ouhte to sperie" (68-69), none of which he does. But then we see where his thoughts have been leading, for they have a clear import. Will may appear bumbling, but his creator has made him a good satirist:

> Ac sythe bondemen barnes haen be mad bisshopes
> And barnes bastardus haen be erchedekenes
> And soutares and here sones for suluer had be knyhtes ...
> Lyf-holynesse and loue hath be longe hennes,
> And wol, til hit be wered out, or oþerwyse ychaunged.
>
> (70-72, 80-81)

His behavior, that is, reflects the behavior of his society, a society under the domination of Meed, even though he himself knows better. Like Isaiah, the "man of unclean lips" dwelling "in the midst of a people that hath unclean lips," Will has kept silent about the corruption he recognizes, and he claims that all that Christ demands is "Preyeres of a parfit man and penaunce discret" (84), an argument that is instantly dismissed by Conscience: "By Crist, y can nat se this lyeth ..." (89).

Conscience's objection is supported later in the poem in the plowing scene when certain "faytours" or "lorelles" (which may recall Will's description of himself as a "lollare") tell Piers

> "And we praye for 30w, Peres, and for 30ure plouh bothe
> That god for his grace 30ure grayn multiplye
> And 3elde 30w of 30ure almesse þat 3e 3euen vs here.
> We may nother swynke ne swete, suche sekenes vs ayleth,
> Ne none lymes to labory with, lord god we thonketh."
>
> (VIII.131-35)

These fakers and malingerers, who appear to thank God that they lack limbs with which to work in the field, are like Will in their attempt to escape from deeds "þat to þe comune nedeth," and they are quickly rebuffed by Piers:

> "3oure preyeres ... and 3e parfyt weren,
> Myhte helpe, as y hope, ac hey Treuthe wolde
> That no faytrye were founde in folk þat goth a-beggeth."
>
> (VIII.136-38)

Similarly Conscience tells Will

> "Ac it semeth no sad parfitnesse in citees to begge,
> But he be obediencer to prior or to mynistre."
>
> (V.90-91)

Even if such begging is a proper form of life, it must be done according to the rules; but even more important, Conscience has questioned whether Will is that "parfit man" whose prayers are so efficacious.

What follows is Will's "conversion." He acknowledges the justice of Conscience's objection, recognizes that he has been wasting his time ("and so y beknowe/That y have ytynt tyme and tyme myspened," 92-93), and expresses the hope

> "to haue of hym þat is almyghty
> A gobet of his grace, and bigynne a tyme
> That alle tymes of my tyme to profit shal turne."
>
> (99-101)

Now he accepts his responsibility to act for the common profit; and though he never tells us precisely what he will do, the clear implication is that he will speak out against Meed and against corruption, the evils that he saw in his first vision — in short, that he will adopt a prophetic stance, that he will write *Piers Plowman*, a prophetic work intended for the common profit.[2] Both Reason and Conscience encourage him in his new resolve, so that he hurries off to church and promptly falls asleep. We may want to laugh at his somnolence, or condemn him for it, but we would surely be more nearly correct to see his second dream representing the beginning of his response to Reason and Conscience.[3]

It may legitimately be asked how we know that the writing of the poem is Will's response to this confrontation. Nowhere does he explicitly say that this is the case. Nonetheless, his resolve to do something that is simultaneously for the common profit and for the salvaging of his own personal time is so strong that we are justified in looking for some concrete result, and the most obvious thing he produces is the poem. This view is supported by another change that Langland made from the B- to the C-Text. In B, Ymagenatif tells Will

> "And þow medlest þee wiþ makynges and my3test go
> seye þi sauter,
> And bidde for hem þat 3yuep þee breed, for þer bokes
> y[n]owe
> To telle men what dowel is, dobet and dobest boþe,
> And prechours to preuen what it is of many a peire freres."
>
> (B.XII.16-19)

The omission of these lines from C indicates a number of points. First, saying the Psalter, like saying prayers for the dead, though praiseworthy, is not enough, and we could not have the new opening to Passus V if these lines were allowed to stand. And second, while there may be enough books and preachers to clarify the meanings of Dowel, Dobet, and Dobest, those books have not had the desired effect, since neither Will nor his society seems to have profited from them. Ecclesiastes may say "Of making many books there is no end," but that line itself comes at the end of a book. If Will has indeed had a vision that he can turn to the common profit, then he is obligated to share that vision, which is what he does in *Piers Plowman*; and what he learns in Passus V requires the omission of these lines from B in the C-Text. Thus, his hurrying to the church where he has his next dream may recall Isaiah's vision in the Temple and perhaps Ezekiel's visionary trip to the Jerusalem Temple, both of which resulted in additional prophetic teaching.

Furthermore, it would seem that making such verses is not an entirely new experience for him but simply one that now has some sanction. Passus V begins

> Thus y awakede, woet god, whan y wonede in Cornehull,
> Kytte and y in a cote, yclothed as a lollare,
> And lytel ylet by, leueth me for sothe,
> Amonges lollares of Londone and lewede ermytes,
> For y made of tho men as resoun me tauhte.
>
> (1-5)

Will is little esteemed by his rough Cornhill neighbors, for he has already been making verses about them, just as Reason was about to encourage him to do. That he has received no honor for these verses is hardly surprising, "For Jesus himself gave testimony that a prophet hath no honor in his own country" (John 4:44). It is not surprising, then, that he makes no mention of such verses when he tells Reason about his activities. They have brought him no honor and he does not seem to recognize their value, just as Isaiah expresses remorse over his silence, although we have already read five chapters of his prophecies. But by the end of this autobiographical episode he knows that he has a calling to begin the life "þat is louable and leele to thy soule" (103), to write *Piers Plowman*. He knows that his verses are not a sign of his idleness, that they are in fact the work that he can do for the "common profit." (And we know, from the A-, B-, and C-Texts that Langland did indeed work at his poem!)

An examination of the autobiographical lines in Passus V, then, in light of the prophetic calls to prophecy, especially that of Isaiah, helps to establish the analogy between prophecy and the kind of poetry Langland was writing and clarifies the nature and subject of that poetry.

3. ISAIAH IN PIERS PLOWMAN

In composing his poem, Langland drew on all the major and some of the minor prophets. We can see the personal narrative of Jeremiah and the startling images and transitions of Ezekiel, but the prophet on whom Langland relied most heavily, and with good reason, was Isaiah. In their general prologue on the prophets, the translators of the Wyclif Bible listed three rules for understanding prophecy:

> The firste is this, that the principal entent of the profetis is to declare the mysterie of Cristis incarnacioun, passioun, resurrecioun, ascensioun, and the comyng to the general doom, and the pupplischyng of the gospel, and the conuercioun of hethene men, and the tribulacioun of hooli chirche in this lijf, and the blis of heuene therfor. The secounde reule is this, that the profetis warnen the puple of Jewis of her grete synnes, and exciten hem to do penaunce . . . The thridde reule is this, that the profetis rehersen ofte benefices 30uun of God bifor to the Jewis. . . .
>
> (III. 225-26)

Of course these three rules apply to all of the literary prophets, but they apply most clearly to Isaiah, especially the first, that which deals with the prophetic announcements of the life and mission of Christ, for Isaiah contains the most and the clearest of those biblical passages that were understood Christologically. As the English translators say, quoting Jerome's prologue to Isaiah, "Isaye is worthi to be seid not onely a profete, but more, a gospellere, for he declarith so opynli the mysteries of Crist and of hooli chirche, that thou gesse hym not oneli to ordeyne a profesie of thing to comynge, but to ordein a storie of thingis passid" (III.225). Here we see not only Isaiah's Christology, but also that obliteration of time that so characterizes medieval Bible commentary. Because of their allegorical approach, the commentators, unless they are focusing expressly on the literal level, can see in a single passage a variety of levels of meaning involving a variety of temporal settings. Probably the best example of this in *Piers Plowman* comes late in the poem when Abraham, Moses, and the Samaritan appear together, in the context of the story of Christ. Just as in the prophets, as they were read in the Middle Ages, all sense of time's reality is obliterated. Everything happens in an atemporal universe. Time becomes like the undifferentiated background in a medieval painting. The Christology of Isaiah makes this technique most striking.

There are other aspects of Isaiah that make it an important source for *Piers Plowman* as well. Individually the items that follow may be regarded as circumstantial, but taken as a whole they seem to form a pattern that points to Langland's use of Isaiah. For example, Isaiah is mentioned by name more than any of the other prophets (except for David) and seems to have represented the idea of prophecy to Langland. Thus, we read that the penitent thief was saved before "Adam oþer Ysaye oþer eny of the profetes" (XI.259), and when Elde shakes the Tree of Charity and the devil gathers the fruit, the fruits are named

"Adam and Abraham and Ysaye þe prophete" (XVIII.113). At first glance it may seem that Isaiah is just a convenient name to use for the alliteration, but Ezekiel, Amos, and Osee would also have been appropriate. Significantly, still in Passus XVIII, while speaking of the Incarnation, the narrator says

> Ac *Liberum Arbitrium* lechecraft hym tauhte
> Til *plenitudo temporis* hy tyme aprochede,
> That suche a surgien sethen ysaye was þer neuere . . .
>   (XVIII.138-40)

It is important to see here not only the prominent place given to Isaiah, but also the close relationship between Isaiah and Christ, who are both described as physicians. This recognition of the similar roles of Isaiah and Christ as healers of their societies, however great the differences between them, lies, as we shall see, behind the whole concept of *Piers Plowman*.

Another reflection of Isaiah in the poem can be seen in some of the names that are used. It is true that Hosea gives the children of his allegorical marriage allegorical names, Without mercy and Not my People (Hosea 1:6,9), and the Ezekiel makes an elaborate allegory out of the names Oolla and Ooliba (She who has a tent and My tent is in her); but Isaiah goes even further. Of course he announces the name of Emmanuel (God is with us, 7:14), and he gives the name of the special child whose birth he predicts as "Wonderful, Counsellor, God the Mighty, the Father of the world to come, the Prince of Peace" (9:6). While these names were obviously interpreted Christologically, Isaiah also gave allegorical names to his children. His son was called in Hebrew Shear-jashub, which means "a remnant shall return" (though Jerome translated the verse "Go forth to meet Ahaz, you and Shear-jashub your son . . ." as "Egredere . . . tu et qui derelictus est Iasub, filius tuus," so that the son's name appears to be simply Jasub). A second son, however, is given the even stranger name of "Hasten to take away the spoils: Make haste to take away the prey." Such names call to mind the names of Piers's family members, his wife "Worch-when-tyme-is, his daughter Do-righte-so-or-thy-dame-shal-þe-bete, and his son Soffre-thy-souereynes-haue-her-wille-Deme-hem-nat-yf-thou-doest-thow-shalt-hit-dere -abygge. If Isaiah's family and Piers's family are not related, there is at least a nominal resemblance.[4]

Yet another way in which Langland relied on Isaiah was for some of his personifications. Not all of them can be found in the prophet, but I do not think it is stretching the point to see some of them there. For example, in Passus XX we see, following the Passion, the well-known debate among the Four Daughters of God, Mercy, Truth, Righteousness, and Peace, followed by the words of Book. Pearsall (325) cites as sources for the Four Daughters Psalm 84:11 ("Mercy and truth have met each other: justice and peace have kissed") and Isaiah 43:5-6 ("I will bring thy seed from the east, and gather thee from the west. I will say to the north: Give up: and to the south: keep not back . . ."), and Travers has cited many post-biblical sources. Surely Pearsall and Travers are correct, and yet if they can find the source in such disparate works, there is yet another relevant passage to consider that might have contributed to this section of the poem. Isaiah 26, part of the so-called "Isaiah Apocalypse," begins, "In die illa cantabitur canticum istud in terra Iuda: Urbs fortitudinis nostrae Sion; salvator ponetur in ea/Murus et ante murate," which in the Wyclif Bible is rendered, "In that day shul be sungen this song in the land of Juda. The huge cite of oure strengthe Sion; a saveour shal be set in it, the wal and the bifor walling." This passage, foreshadowing the Crucifixion that opens Passus XX, introduces the canticle, which includes the following verses: "2. Openeth the 3ates, and there shall go in a ri3twis folc, kepende *treuthe*. 3. The olde errour 3ide awei; thou shalt kepe *pes, pes*, for in thee, Lord, wee han hopid. . . . 9. My soule shal desire thee in ny3t, but and with my spirit in my herte inward thingus; for erly I shal wake to thee. Whan thou shalt don thi domes in the erthe, *ri3twisnesse* shul lernen alle the dwelleris of the world. 10. Have wee *mercy* to the unpitouse, and he shal not lerne to do ri3twisnesse; in the lond of halewis wicke thingus he dide, and he shal not see the glorie of the Lord" (italics added). In these verses the four qualities are mentioned in a context more pertinent to Passus XX, following the reference to a savior in Sion and preceding a reference to resurrection: "19. Lyuen shul thi deade, my slayne men shuln a3een rise. . . ." Langland has taken this passage, in which these qualities are more active than in the psalm cited by Pearsall, and made of them speaking characters who discuss the Crucifixion and the resurrection of the dead.

The passage from Isaiah becomes even more clearly relevant if we notice the note in the Wyclif Bible that defines Sion as "heuenli citee, whois excellence mai not be declarid bi mannus wordis," which makes "Openeth the 3ates, and there shal go in ri3twis folc" refer specifically to the Daughters' conversation about the possibility of the righteous dead entering heaven. As Pearsall notes, "It is unusual for the debate to be placed at this point in the Christian story, between the Passion and the Harrowing of Hell" (324), but it seems that Langland's reading of Isaiah 26 makes this placement of the debate quite appropriate. In addition, Langland's version of the debate is not on the same apocalyptic plane that most versions occupy. This is not in the least to argue against Psalm 84 as the primary source of this episode, especially since Langland actually quotes from the psalm later in Passus XX (467a). It is, rather, an attempt to show that Langland's use of the psalm was also influenced, however slightly, by the passage in Isaiah. Given medieval notions about the seamlessness of the biblical text, the verbal concordance between the passage in Psalms and that in Isaiah could easily have led Langland to conflate them.

Nor does Langland's use of Isaiah in this passus end here, for the Daughters' conversation is interrupted by the speech of Book. R. E. Kaske has traced the sources of Book's speech through commentaries on Matthew 2 and Psalm 18

(35ff.), but it may still be asked why this speech is delivered by a character called Book. We can find the answer in Isaiah 29: "11. And the vision of all shall be unto you as the words of a book that is sealed. 12. And the book shall be given to one that knoweth no letters, and it shall be said to him: Read: and he shall answer: I know no letters." Then, after four verses condemning people who mouth the law but do not obey it (another of Langland's favorite points), the prophet announces a time when Lebanon will be turned into a fruitful field (v. 15) and then he declares: "18. And in that day the deaf shall hear the words of the book, and out of darkness and obscurity the eyes of the blind shall see." These lines are clearly related to Book's speech, which ends by condemning those Jews who persist in being deaf and blind to the New Law. To the Jews the Book is as though sealed, or they cannot read it; but finally even they will understand it. Thus Book closes his speech by saying

> 'And ȝut y, Boek, wol be brente bote he aryse to lyue
> And comforte alle his kyn and out of care brynge
> And alle þe Iewene ioye vnioynen and vnlouken,
> And bote they reuerense this resurexioun and þe rode
>   honoure
> And bileue on a newe lawe, be ylost lyf and soule.'
>   (XX.264-68)

There is yet one more borrowing in Passus XX from Isaiah. Just before the debate and after the Passion, we read

> Thenne gan Faith fouely þe false Iewes to dispice
> Calde hem caytyues, acorsed for euere:
> 'For þis was a vyl vilanye; vengeaunce ȝow bifall
> That made þe blynde bete the dede — this was a boyes
>   dede! ...
> And alle ȝoure childerne, cherles, cheue shall neuere,
> Ne haue lordschipe in londe ne no londe tulye....'
>   (XX.96-99, 108-09)

Faith-Abraham, who has recently behaved badly compared to the Samaritan, suddenly berates the Jews for their involvement in the Crucifixion. We shall deal later with the reasons for Langland's frequent use of the Jews as targets, but here it is sufficient to point to the source of Abraham's apparent disavowal of the Jews in Isaiah 63:16. Again, following a Christological passage that shows Christ's triumph, we read, "For thou art our father, and Abraham hath not known us. . . ." Again Langland takes a passage from Isaiah and develops it within the context of his own poem, thereby aligning himself with the prophetic voice. Passus XX, then, draws much of its substance from the prophet Isaiah.

There are also in *Piers Plowman* a number of simpler verbal echoes from Isaiah. One that seems quite striking comes at the end of Passus XVII, when Liberum Arbitrium urges priests to try to teach Jews and Saracens about Christianity:

> Prelates and prestes sholde preue yf they myhte
> Lere hem littelum and littelum *et in Jesum Christum filium,*
> Til they couthe speke and spele *et in Spiritum sanctum,*
> Recorden hit and rendren hit with *remissionem*
> peccatorum. . . .
>
> (XVII.319-22)

This passage, especially in the peculiar phrase "littelum and littelum" recalls a similar passage in Isaiah that is also about teaching:

> Et erit eis verbum Domini:
> Manda, remanda; manda, remanda;
> Exspecta, reexspecta; exspecta, reexspecta;
> Modicum ibi, modicum ibi.
>
> (28:13)

While "Modicum ibi, modicum ibi" is usually translated "little by little," Langland's "littelum and littelum" seems to be a clear verbal echo of the prophet.

In addition to such verbal echoes, there are, of course, clearer and more extended references to Isaiah in *Piers Plowman.* For example, Conscience says

> "Ac Kynde loue shal come Ꝫut and Consience togyderes
> And maky of lawe a laborer, suche loue shal aryse
> And such pees among þe peple and a parfit treuthe,
> That Iewes shal wene in her wit and wexen so glade
> That here kyng be ycome fro þe court of heuene,
> That ilk Moises or Messie, þat men ben so trewe.
> For alle þat bereth baslard, briht swerd oþer launce,
> Ax oþer hachet or eny kyne wypne,
> Shal be demed to þe deth but yf he do hit smythye
> Into sykel or into sythe, to shar oþer to coltur."
>
> (III.451-60)

Obviously the last four lines here are taken from Isaiah 2:4, "and they shall turn their swords into ploughshares, and their spears into sickles . . ." and yet Langland has not just copied the prophet's words. He expands and transforms them. Where Isaiah mentions swords and spears, Langland speaks of baslards,

swords, lances, hatchets, and other weapons; and where Isaiah mentions ploughshares and sickles, Langland speaks of sickles, scythes, ploughshares, and coul-
ters. Furthermore, whereas Isaiah describes what appears to be an ideal,
peaceful state, Langland feels compelled to say that not everyone will fit in, and
those who do not will be condemned to death. As in the debate of the Four
Daughters of God, Langland is not simply copying the words of Isaiah, and Isaiah
is not a solitary source for Langland. Rather, in adopting a prophetic stance,
Langland makes them his own. Isaiah gives him a starting point, but he develops
his own trains of thought. Thus in Passus VIII, Piers says:

> "For y wol sowen hit mysulf and sethe wol y wende
> To pilgrimages, as palmeres doen, pardon to wynne.
> My plouh pote shal be my pyk-staff and pyche a-to þe rotes
> And helpe my coltur to kerue and clanse þe forwes."
>   (VIII.62-5)

As the act of plowing becomes the pilgrimage, the weapons that have been made
into farm implements become the tools of the pilgrim, thereby embodying one
of Langland's main themes, the religious requirement of active participation in
the world for the common profit.

If all of this comes from III.457-60, the preceding lines illustrate yet another
way in which Langland uses Isaiah, for they include a kind of messianic foretelling reminiscent of the Christological passages in Isaiah, including those in
chapter 2. What he says here, furthermore, is not just a repetition of Isaiah's
foreshadowing of Christ. Rather he says that when Kynde Love and Conscience
rule together, the times will be so good, the commonalty will function so well,
that even the Jews will think the Messiah has come. What will bring this all
about is the ability of Kynde Love and Conscience to "maky of lawe a laborer."
This strange phrase is easily understood after a look at Isaiah 2:3: "And many
people shall go, and say: Come and let us go up to the mountain of the Lord,
and to the house of the God of Jacob, and he will teach us his ways, and we will
walk in his paths: for the law shall come forth from Sion, and the word of the
Lord from Jerusalem." The law will come forth — for Langland, it had already
come forth; but seeing the corruption around him, he felt that it was not working.
But Kynde Love and Conscience have the power to make it work, to make it a
laborer, so that we may learn "his ways" and "walk in his paths."

What Langland has done here is to use the writings of Isaiah — the prophet's
words, his themes, his ideas — to reflect on his own times. To do so he has
juxtaposed various prophecies, expanded or contracted them, made them his
own, because of his own deeply felt prophetic urges in relation to his own time.
There is really nothing odd about this procedure; if biblical history is an on-going
affair, then the biblical patterns and themes maintain their relevance. This is,
as we saw, one of the bases of Joachimist thought. If, for Joachim, the Old

Testament is the key to history (Bloomfield 1957, 264-65), then so it may be for Langland as well. We can see this idea most clearly in Langland's startling use of Isaiah's first chapter.

If Langland, as we saw in looking at Passus XX, can adapt a variety of passages from Isaiah to structure his poem, he can also rely on the prophet in another way, as we can see in his use of Isaiah as a basis for the Visio section of *Piers Plowman*. The very word "visio," of course, recalls the prophets. Obadiah begins, "Visio Abdiae," and Nahum begins, "Onus Ninive. Liber visionis Nahum Elcesaei." In the first verse of Ezekiel we read "et vidi visiones Dei" and the first words of Isaiah are "Visio Isaiae." Thus whoever provided such titles as "Visio Willelmi de Petro Plouhman" or "visio eiusdem Willelmi de Dowel," whether it was the author or a scribe, recognized the poem's relationship to the prophets. And at first glance, the beginning of *Piers* slightly resembles the opening of Ezekiel. Ezekiel begins by telling where and when he saw the vision, just as Will does. Moreover, Will's vision, like Ezekiel's, is a very visual one: both of them see scenes that they describe in detail and that the reader can consequently visualize.[5]

While it may seem odd to say that these visions are visual, they both stand in contrast to Isaiah's opening vision, which consists largely of a variety of metaphors in which Isaiah announces his basic themes of the people's sinfulness, the need for repentance, and God's assured forgiveness. Since these are also among Langland's basic themes, the opening of *Piers Plowman* presents a fascinating amalgamation of Ezekiel's visual quality and Isaiah's imagery. Langland produces this amalgamation by a technique we have seen him use elsewhere, the expansion, often in great detail, of an image that he finds in the Bible. For example, near the beginning of Isaiah 1 we read:

> 3. The ox knoweth his owner and the ass his master's crib: but Israel hath not known me, and my people hath not understood. 4. Woe to the sinful nation, a people laden with iniquity, a wicked seed, ungracious children: they have forsaken the Law, they have blasphemed the Holy One of Israel, they are gone away backwards. 5. For what shall I strike you any more, you that increase transgressions? the whole head is sick, and the whole heart is sad. 6. From the sole of the foot unto the top of the head, there is no soundness therein. . . .

These are surely striking images, moving from the pastoral image of the ox and the ass to the metaphor of the whole people as a human body, a body that is diseased in its head and in its heart, from the bottom to the top. Langland, who sees the same problems in his society, expands on Isaiah's words in his very specific description of the fair field full of folk. In order to convey the sense that the entire "body" of England is diseased, he uses estates satire to survey that body from bottom to top, from plowmen (Prol.22) to the king (Prol.139). Between those extremes, he illustrates how every part of the "body" is diseased. We see the corruption of minstrels, beggars, pilgrims, friars, pardoners, priests, lawyers, and ultimately even the king. Isaiah tells us that his society is corrupt; Langland shows us that his is.

Isaiah also tells us how his society is corrupt. It places far too much emphasis on the externals of religious observance, on the rituals, making an artificial distinction between religious and moral behavior:

> 11. To what purpose do you offer me the multitude of your
> victims, saith the Lord? I am full, I desire not holocausts of
> rams, and fat of fatlings, and blood of calves, and lambs,
> and buck goats. 12. When you came to appear before me,
> who required these things at your hands, that you should
> walk in my courts? 13. Offer sacrifices no more in vain: in-
> cense is an abomination to me. The new moons, and the
> sabbaths, and other festivals I will not abide, your as-
> semblies are wicked. 14. My soul hateth your new moons,
> and your solemnities: they are become troublesome to me,
> I am weary of bearing them.

Langland's Prologue is full of similar condemnations of such easy, superficial religious observance. He attacks those pilgrims who profess to travel for religious reasons but whose religiosity is false. They

> Wenten forth on here way with many wyse tales
> And hadde leue to lye aftir, al here lyf-tyme.
> (Prol. 49-50).

As we see elsewhere in the poem, such pilgrims make a show of their piety, which is, in reality, as empty as the sacrifices cited by Isaiah. Their religiosity is all show and no substance. Similarly, the friars present an image of piety, but they preach for their own profit and "glosede the gospel as hem good likede" (Prol. 58), as a result of which "charite hath be chapman and chief to shryue lordes" (Prol. 62). What they call charity is nothing more than an excuse for them to continue their immoral behavior, just as the empty sacrifices cited by Isaiah are used to justify the immoral behavior that he attacks.

Langland's attack on the pardoner is similar. The pardoner promises that he can absolve people "Of falsnesses of fastynges, of vowes ybrokene" (Prol. 69) and the people flock to him because he offers an easy solution to their sinfulness. His absolution requires no inward feeling, no true repentance. It is superficial, an empty ritual. So, too, the parish priests, while maintaining the outward trappings of the priesthood, have abandoned its real function, which is "charite to tylie" (Prol. 87) and instead concern themselves with political economics. They work for the king, he says, "And summe aren as seneschalles and seruen oþer lordes" (Prol. 93). On one level, obviously, Langland is referring to other lords of the realm, but we cannot ignore the prophetic note in the phrase "seruen oþer lordes," for Israel's attraction to other lords is a constant cause of complaint in the prophets. Isaiah says, "The ox knoweth his owner and the ass his master's crib: but Israel hath not known me" and later "they shall be confounded for the idols, to which they have sacrificed . . ." (1:29). Lest anyone miss the correspondence, Langland added to the C-Text Conscience's attack:

> "Ydolatrie ȝe soffren in sondrye places manye
> And boxes ben yset forth ybounde with yren
> To vndertake þe tol of vntrewe sacrefice."
>
> (Prol. 96-98)

Then, after comparing contemporary priests to Ophni and Phinees, the first of Langland's applications of biblical personages to contemporary life, Conscience, sounding like Isaiah, adds

> "ȝoure masse and ȝour matynes and many of ȝoure oures
> Ar don vndeuouteliche. . . ."
>
> (Prol. 125-26)

Indeed, all along Conscience has been speaking in a prophetic voice, angry, condemning the corruption he sees, but not proclaiming punishment so much as seeking repentance:

> "Forthy y sey ȝe prestes and men of holy churche
> That soffreth men do sacrefyce and worschipe
>   maumettes . . .
> God shal take vengeaunce on alle suche prestis . . ."
>
> (Prol. 118-19, 121)

Langland's use of Isaiah to give shape to the prologue is quite clear. At this point, however, Langland seems to abandon the prophet, though as we shall see he is simply digressing in order to make his point more effectively, for he now introduces two people who have the power to reform society, the Pope and the King; but he also shows their lack of effectiveness, partially, at least, the result of the cardinals and the lawyers. What we see in both cases is an ideal of what can be accomplished in those offices:

> I parsceyued of þe power that Peter hadde to kepe,
> To bynde and to vnbynde, as þe boke telleth . . .
> Myght of tho men made hym to regne.
> And thenne cam Kynde Wytt and clerkus he made
> And Conscience and Kynde Wit and knyghthed togedres
> Caste þat þe comunes sholde here comunes fynde.
>   (Prol. 128-29, 139-43)

It is important to understand here that "comune" generally refers to the com-monwealth or the community (Donaldson 94ff.), for so much of what Langland says deals with the life of the community. What Langland describes here seems like an ideal human community, in which the upper classes work together in an orderly way to allow the commonwealth to provide for itself. In doing so, they will discover not only their provisions (one meaning of "comunes") but their common-ness, their interdependence. Of course such an ideal state is neces-sarily shortlived, thanks, in this instance, to the lawyers.

The kinds of problems Langland has been discussing are exemplified in the fable of the rats and the mice. Whatever contemporary allusions may be buried in the fable, the main point is that the community of rodents is being threatened and it therefore behooves all to act for the "comune profit," a phrase that recurs several times in the fable. When they arrive at a solution to their problem that they find is difficult to carry out, the mouse makes a remarkable speech in which he says, "y conseile for oure comune profit lat þe cat yworthe" (Prol. 201). Because the solution is difficult, the mouse suggests that it is in the common interest to ignore the problem. Suddenly the idea of common profit has been stood on its head; and the mouse's further advice, that the rodents take no action whatever "But soffre and say nouȝt" (Prol. 211) is an argument for inaction in the face of public danger. This, as we shall see in Passus I, and throughout *Piers Plowman*, is a stance that Langland could not accept. That this tale applies to England is clear from the reference to Ecclesiastes, "Ve terre ubi puer est Rex," but the real problem here is not the child-king so much as it is the kind of commonwealth that accepts the mouse's advice, and Langland concludes the passus by returning us to a picture of that commonwealth.

What we see in the Prologue, then, is Langland, through Will, adopting a prophetic stance, conveying his vision of a corrupt society by adapting the terms of Isaiah's vision, describing the possibility of an ideal society, and then showing the obstacles that prevent that ideal from becoming reality. In Passus I, he continues to use this prophetic stance. He begins by telling us that he will explain his earlier allegory, just as the prophets explain their allegorical visions (after the Song of Vineyard in Isaiah 5, Isaiah says, "For the vineyard of the Lord of hosts is the house of Israel: and the man of Juda his pleasant plant . . ."), or as Jesus explains the parables, in what Hugh of St.-Cher describes as one step in prophecy; but Will explains this allegory with the help of Holy Church. While many of Will's instructors are psychological allegories, Holy Church is not one of them. Rather, she is a kind of divine spokeswoman, which makes him an intermediary, revealing divine truths to an earthly audience, just as the prophets did.[6] His fear at seeing her, too, although it may have been influenced by Boethius, recalls the reaction of Isaiah and Ezekiel at their calls. Holy Church's divine role is further supported when she provides what Sister Rose Bernard Donna calls "the key to the understanding of the Vision of William concerning Piers the Plowman" (v). If people could understand what Holy Church says, the rest of the poem would not be necessary; but what Holy Church says, while it appears simple and straightforward, is difficult indeed. In the middle of their conversation, Will suddenly asks Holy Church

> "Teche me to no tresor, but telle me this ilke,
> How y may saue my soule, þat saynt art yholde."
>
> (I.79-80)

Again Pearsall is correct in seeing the question as a reflection of the rich young man's question in Matthew 19:16, but what is really important here is Holy Church's answer, and that answer is derived from Isaiah. Holy Church tells Will

> "For who is trewe of his tonge and of his two handes
> And doth þe werkes þerwith and wilneth no man ylle,
> He is a god by þe gospel and graunte may hele
> And also lyke oure lord, by saynt Lukes wordes."
>
> (I.84-87)

Holy Church's answer recalls a passage from Isaiah 1 that we examined much earlier: "16. Wash yourselves, be clean, take away the evil of your devices from my eyes: cease to do perversely, 17. Learn to do well: seek judgment, relieve the oppressed, judge for the fatherless, defend the widow." The answer to Will's question is that simple: he may save his soul by ceasing to do evil ("wilneth no man ylle") and learning to do well ("doth þe werkes"). The problem is to know what those words mean. What does it mean "to do perversely" and, perhaps more important, what does it mean "to do well"?[7] Isaiah seems to explain, but the things he mentions — seeking judgment, caring for the weak and oppressed — are really examples rather than explanations. What is important, however, is the emphasis on doing. The examples he gives all require active doing, and this is essential for understanding *Piers Plowman*, in which Dowel, Dobet, and Dobest play such prominent parts, in which Holy Church tells Will that that person will be saved who "doth þe werkes."

Although I shall examine the implications of Langland's prophetic stance on the "Do" triad later, a word about them is in order now. Many fine scholars have investigated Dowel, Dobet, and Dobest, and they have found many ingenious and enlightening explanations for those terms; but their focus has almost always been on the "wel," "bet," and "best" parts. Those parts must certainly be understood, and I will offer my own explanations later; but perhaps the primary focus should be on the "Do" parts of those terms. The words of Holy Church, buttressed by the words of Isaiah, all emphasize the need for action, and even the rich young man in Matthew says, "What shall I do . . . ?" For Langland, in his prophetic frame of mind, England was in trouble; and if part of the problem was that many people, like those in the Prologue, were actively pursuing evil, another part of the problem was that too many people were, like the mouse, not actively pursuing solutions. The solutions were there — they had been taught by the Church — and they could be summarized in the phrase "do well." But what does that mean? Much of the rest of *Piers Plowman* is an attempt to explain.

If this seems like a simple approach to *Piers Plowman*, perhaps it is; but one of the implications of Langland's prophetic stance is that he was trying to change his society and the individuals that constituted it, and therefore that he was trying to communicate to them what he understood as some basic truths. These truths had to be accessible, and the events of 1381 show that many people thought them to be so. George Kane has suggested that "Some Langland scholarship seems too recondite, suggesting (if not intentionally) that the significant communication of *Piers Plowman* is accessible only to special kinds of erudition not primarily literary in our modern sense" (1981, 6). Such criticism is reminiscent of Kierkegaard's criticism of biblical criticism that we saw earlier. Langland's significant communication — learn to do well, to do better, to do best — is not so difficult to understand, though it continues to be difficult to do. Rather than confronting it, however, too often "we shield ourselves by hiding behind tomes." Consequently, the important things that Langland was saying to his society — and to ours — are lost.

Having defended my simple approach to the poem, I will now contradict myself. Isaiah is clear about what he expects — cease to do perversely, learn to do well — and Langland is clear about what he expects — be true of tongue and of hands, do the works and will no man ill. But despite their apparent simplicity, these are not simple concepts. What does it mean to do well or to be true of tongue? If this is Isaiah's main point and he makes it in the first chapter, why do we need another sixty-five chapters? One answer is so that we can try to understand what it means to do well and to see the implications of our doing well and doing evil. Similarly, Langland wants us to understand, so that if the "Visio" is inspired by Isaiah 1, the "Vitae" are based in large part on Isaiah 1:17-18, "Et venite, et arguite me, dicit Dominus." Verse 18 is translated in the RSV as "Come now, let us reason together, says the Lord," but the Hebrew appears to say, more precisely, "Let us discuss" or "Let us argue." "Arguite," the word Jerome uses, means "show, demonstrate, make clear" and is a word often used in the legal sense of accusing. In the Wyclif Bible the word is translated as "vndernemeth mee" or "repreue 3e me," and the gloss on this phrase reads, "that is, if 3e doen these thingis, thanne 3e moun playne, if 3e ben not releeuyd of God (III.228)." This is also the sense of the Douay-Reims translation, "And then come, and accuse me, saith the Lord."

Nonetheless, I would argue that Langland understood the word in the non-legal sense of "make clear" or "prove," possibly in conjunction with "argumentor," which involves reason and discussion and is therefore closer to the Hebrew. I make such a point of this because, obviously, the "Vitae" consist largely of a series of discussions and arguments, some more reasoned than others, on precisely what it means to do well, better, and best. Furthermore, the next part of the verse in Isaiah is clearly relevant to *Piers Plowman*: "if your sins be as scarlet, they shall be made as white as snow: and if they be red as crimson, they shall be white as wool." The second section of *Piers Plowman*, then, is a working out of the meaning of "learn to do well." It shows Langland, through Will, taking up the invitation of Isaiah 1:18, "venite et arguite me," so that the people's repentance, for which he, with his prophetic voice, is calling, may be effective, so that their sins, and his own, may be purified.

This discussion of doing well, however, must wait, for Langland is not yet finished with Isaiah 1. If the poet was critical of all the classes in society, as he appeared to be in the Prologue, he was especially critical of the ruling classes, both lay and ecclesiastical, for corrupting the people by not performing their roles properly. Isaiah 1:23 reads, "Thy princes are faithless, companions of thieves: they all love bribes, they run after rewards. They judge not for the fatherless: and the widow's cause cometh not in to them." The later version of the Wyclif Bible renders the middle section of this verse "alle louen 3iftes, suen meedis." This verse is one source of Passus II, III, and IV, the story of Lady Meed.[8] We have already seen Langland expanding on his prophetic sources, though not to this extent. Obviously he thought that bribery was an important contemporary problem, and, relying on the history of Lady Meed (for which, see Yunck), he developed this narrative section that allows him to discuss her nature, to illustrate her influence, and to bring in a number of other prophetic themes.

It is obvious at the beginning of Meed's story that she is a powerful woman, both "In kynges court" and "In þe popes palays" (II.22-23) as well as in other levels of society, judging by the knights, clerks, jurymen, summoners, merchants, and others who are invited to her wedding. In fact the whole story of Lady Meed, with Simony and Civil Law going to Rome and with the events at Westminster, illustrates the level of corruption in both the secular and religious spheres; and Langland's surveys of his corrupt society (e.g., III.79-83) remind us of Amos' condemnation, "For three crimes of Israel, and for four I will not convert him: because he has sold the just man for silver, and the poor man for a pair of shoes" (2:6). Langland's picture of English life through most of Passus II, III, and IV makes vivid, in considerable detail, the words of Isaiah in 1:24, "How is the faithful city, that was full of judgment, become a harlot? justice dwelt in it, but now murderers." Langland is not concerned so much with murder as with other perversions of justice, but Meed is clearly the harlot who typifies what the city has become, and in fact at her fall

> Mede mornede tho and made an hevy chere,
> For þe comune calde here queynte comune hore.
>
> (IV.160-61)

The episode involving Peace and Wrong illustrates the way Langland relies on Isaiah. Peace accuses Wrong of such crimes as ravishing Rose the widow, murdering his workers, and stealing, all of which reflect sins that are mentioned in Isaiah 1; but Wrong, with the help of lawyers and Meed, almost escapes punishment. One of the wise men argues that if Wrong will only make amends, he should be allowed to go free; and when Meed offers Peace "a present al of puyre golde" (IV.91), Peace prays to the king to let Wrong go. Of course, a gift of gold, not accompanied by true repentance, is not amends. It is a bribe, and it cannot make up for Wrong's misdeeds. Peace, presumably, seeks peaceful solutions, is duped, and Wrong nearly goes free. All of this constitutes an elaborate exemplum of Isaiah 1:21-23. Fortunately, however, Langland also recalls Isaiah 1:26, for after Isaiah's attacks come predictions of reform: "And I will restore thy judges as they were before, and thy counsellors as of old. After this thou shalt be called the city of the just, a faithful city." The king's counsellors in this episode are Reason and Conscience, and the king does indeed condemn Wrong. Furthermore, when Reason is asked to be merciful to Wrong, he makes a long speech (IV.108-32) in which he describes an ideal time and an ideal place like the faithful city of Isaiah 1:26, though even in this clear, uncompromising speech, the clerks, confessor, and lawyers try to find loopholes. The king, who is now something of an ideal king, continues to hold Meed responsible, but Conscience makes the important point that such reforms must involve every level of society:

> Quod Consience to þe kyng, "Withoute þe comune helpe
> Hit is ful hard, by myn heued, herto to bryngen hit
> And alle ȝoure lege lordes to lede thus evene."
>
> (IV.176-78)

Reform may have begun, but one person, even the king, cannot carry it out alone. What Langland is doing here is what the prophets often do, discussing the relationship between individual and communal responsibility, an important theme in *Piers Plowman* to which we shall return.

With this picture of an ideal king initiating reforms, Will awakens, but this does not mark the end of Langland's use of Isaiah 1, for in Passus VI and part of Passus VII we have the confessions of the sins, which recalls the promise in 1:18, "if your sins be as scarlet, they shall be made white as snow: and if they be red as crimson, they shall be white as wool." The Isaiah passage seems relevant to the confession scene largely because of the strangeness of that scene. What, after all, does it mean to say that the sins are confessing? Can they truly confess their sins and repent? When Donne says, "Death, thou shalt die," he expresses the paradox that death itself will die when souls are raised to eternal life. Langland is playing with a similar paradox. If these sins actually repented, they would cease to exist; but clearly they cannot repent, for to repent would be to deny their own essences. We should not, therefore, in our earthly existence, look for the abolition of sin, and Isaiah does not mean that sin will disappear. This scene is clearly not an apocalyptic vision. Rather the prophet is speaking of individual sinfulness, which is quite a different matter and a point with which Langland is frequently concerned. The sins themselves, despite what might be called their best efforts, cannot become "as white as snow." What is required is for individuals, like the individuals cited by the sins, to make their best efforts to repent, to make their own sins "as white as snow" and to resist them in the future. In short, individuals must do what the sins cannot — they must do well — and part of that requires true repentance and restitution. Even Repentance cannot tell when repentance is sincere.

Significantly, the confession of the sins leads to the pilgrimage to Truth, to the plowing of the half-acre, and to the pardon. The pilgrimage and the plowing motifs, with their emphasis on external manifestations of religiosity and the need for widespread reform and cooperation for common profit reflect the thought of Isaiah 1, as we have seen. So, too, does the pardon. The pardon itself seems quite simple:

> *Qui bona egerunt ibunt in vitam eternam;*
> *Qui vero mala in ignem eternum.*
>
> (IX.288-89)

This particular formulation comes from the Athanasian Creed, but it is really little more than a clear formulation of the biblical doctrine of reward and punishment. As such, it is related to Isaiah 1:19-20: "If you be willing, and will hearken to me, you shall eat the good things of the land. But if you will not, and will provoke me to wrath: the sword shall devour you because the mouth of the Lord hath spoken it." This passage reinforces the connection between Passus VIII and IX. Passus VIII ends with the oppression of Hunger and the narrator's prophetic warning of famine, floods, pestilence, and world-wide battle, "But yf god of his goodnesse graunte vs a trewe" (VIII.354). If God forgives the people, presumably as a result of their repentance, they will "eat the good things of the land," but this reward leans heavily on "But yf." (As Will noted earlier, "So god gyueth nothyng þat *si* ne is the glose," [III.328], a good prophetic sentiment.) If they continue to behave as they have in the past, they face famine and death.

Passus IX opens with Piers's attempt, with the aid of the pardon, "to set up the true Christian community" (Pearsall 161), in which kings, knights, and bishops, "yf they ben as they sholde," (IX.14) receive rewards; in which merchants can save themselves by building hospitals, repairing bridges, and caring for the poor; in which even lawyers can be saved by helping the innocent and the poor; in which laborers, deserving beggars, God's minstrels, and true hermits can all be saved. And what is the Pardon that makes this all possible? As the priest translates it

> "Dowel and haue wel and god shal haue thy soule
> And do yuele and haue euele and hope thow non oþere
> Bote he þat euele lyueth euele shal ende."
>
> (IX.291-93)

While these sentiments can be found elsewhere in the Bible, they again reflect the essential words from Isaiah, "cease to do perversely, learn to do well"; and just as Isaiah gives examples of doing well, so Langland has opened the passus with examples and provided a picture of the kind of society that will result from doing well.

The end of Passus IX is especially interesting and buttresses the argument I have been making. Immediately after the priest translates the pardon, Will awakens and discusses the nature of dreams. Many dreams, he acknowledges, have no value, but others, like the prophetic dreams of Daniel and Joseph, do. "Al this," he says, "maketh me on meteles to studie" (IX.319). He recognizes, and wants us to recognize, the prophetic nature of his dream, so that we may be more aware of the nature of Dowel; and Langland closes both Passus IX and the Visio with reflections on Dowel: it transcends other pardons, pilgrimages, "bionales and trionales," bulls and indulgences. It consists of pardon, penance, and prayers (IX.330) and of following the Ten Commandments (IX.336). And the passus ends with his advice that we pray not directly for salvation but

> That god gyue vs grace here ar we go hennes
> Suche werkes to worche the while we ben here
> That aftur oure deth-day Dowel reherce
> At þe day of dome we dede as he tauhte. Amen
>
> (IX.350-54)

We should pray for the opportunity to do well, to perform good works. That would be a sign of God's grace. Langland never looks for the easy way — a divine abolition of sin or the direct, unmediated effects of grace. Such systems make no demands on us, and Langland cannot accept them. Human beings, with the aid of grace, must learn to do well. We can see this point, of course, elsewhere in the Bible, for example in "the Epistle General of James, with its emphasis on the need for good works (and hence on their efficacy) in the scheme of salvation" (Murtaugh 32). As Donna says, "Since Christ has laid down the conditions for the forgiveness of sin, Langland assures us, we have but to fulfill them to be assured of eternal salvation" (160). This is the point of Langland's reliance on Isaiah 1 in the Visio, with its focus on doing well, and the rest of the poem will examine what doing well means for individuals and for societies.

Before we look at the implications of Langland's use of the prophets, there is still other evidence that Langland saw himself operating in a prophetic mode. For instance, more than twenty times in *Piers Plowman*, Langland talks about Jews.[9] This seems odd for someone writing almost a century after the Jews had been expelled from England in 1290. These references to the Jews, to be sure, are not complimentary, dealing as they do with such staples of medieval anti-Semitism as Jewish usury and the role of the Jews in the Crucifixion. Nonetheless, considering that there were virtually no Jews in Langland's England, and certainly none of any historical importance, it might well be asked who the audience was for such passages. These passages, of course, by their very existence recall prophetic attacks on the Hebrews, but in this case they must have been directed at Langland's English, Christian audience, not to reinforce their anti-Semitism but to make a point about their moral and religious states. The prophets frequently rely on comparisons or analogies between the Hebrews and other peoples to make their points. Amos, for instance, prophesies against Damascus, Tyre, Edom, and Moab, all of which may have pleased his Hebrew listeners, but when he includes Judah and Israel in his list, the effect is startling (Amos 1-2). Ezekiel, too, contains prophecies about many other nations, but even more to the point is his allegory of Oolla and Ooliba, Samaria and Jerusalem. Oolla, the elder, becomes a lover of Assyria, sins against God, and is therefore punished. She should, of course, serve as a negative example to her younger sister, but instead of learning from her sister's fate, "When her sister Ooliba saw this, she was mad with lust more than she: and she carried her fornication beyond the fornication of her sister" (23:11). Ooliba's sins are described in far more graphic detail than Oolla's, as is her punishment; and the prophet adds, "Thus saith the Lord God: Thou shalt drink thy sister's cup, deep, and wide: thou shalt be had in derision and scorn, which containeth very much" (23:32). There is no need for Ezekiel to prophesy against Oolla, since Samaria had already been destroyed, but his prophecy against Ooliba can be so vehement because the younger sister has refused to learn from the older sister's experience. Isaiah makes a similar point when he says, "Shall I not, as I have done to Samaria and her idols, so do to Jerusalem and her idols?" (10:11).

Jeremiah casts further light on this question. He is told to stand before the Temple and say, "Trust not in lying words, saying: The temple of the Lord, the temple of the Lord, it is the temple of the Lord. For if you will order well your ways, and your doings: if you will execute judgment between a man and his neighbor, if you oppress not the stranger, the fatherless, and the widow, and shed not innocent blood in this place . . . I will dwell with you in this place" (7:4-7). Jeremiah indicates that the people have come to think of the Temple as a talisman, as their protection against the wrath of God; but Jeremiah's point is that the Temple by itself is merely a pile of rocks, that divorced from well doing (in examples that recall Isaiah) the Temple is worthless.

Taken together, these two motifs, the failure of Judah to learn from the fate of Samaria and the tendency to regard the Temple building, with its ritual significance, as itself protection against destruction, help to explain the prominent use of the Jews in *Piers Plowman*, as Faith-Abraham makes clear when he chastises the Jews:

> "Corsede Caytifues! knyhthoed was hit neuere
> To bete a body ybounde, with eny briht wypene . . .
> . . . ӡe, lordeyns, haen lost, for Lyf shal haue maistrie,
> And ӡoure franchise þat fre was yfallen is into thraldoem,
> And alle ӡoure childerne, cherles, cheue shall neuere,
> Ne haue lordschipe in londe ne no londe tulye,
> And as bareyne be, and by vsure libbe,
> The which is lif þat oure lord in all lawes defendeth."
>   (XX.100-11)

Just as Ezekiel and Isaiah use Samaria as an example to warn Judah, so Langland uses the Jews (and occasionally the Saracens, though the latter were not as well known) to warn the Christians. Faith-Abraham enumerates the punishments that have been visited on the Jews for their refusal to acknowledge the divinity of Christ, but those nominal Christians who pervert Christ's teachings, whose Christianity is as devoid of God's presence as was Jeremiah's image of the Temple, also do not acknowledge the divinity of Christ. Certainly they claim to, but their failure to do well is indicative of the hollowness of their claims. Their kind of Christianity is no more than a sort of talisman, something that they believe will save them without their having to do anything. Their fate, Langland implies, will be like that of the Jews. The Jews, as the audience of the biblical prophets, become an analogue for his audience.

There is also in some of the passages about Jews a sense that if Jews can be faithful to their teachings, how much more should Christians be faithful to theirs:

> Iewes lyuen in þe law þat oure lord tauhte
> Moises to be maister þerof til Messie come,
> And on þat lawe they leue and leten hit for þe beste.
>   (XVII.297-99)

This, too, is a kind of prophetic exhortation along the lines of Isaiah's "The ox knoweth his owner, but Israel hath not known me." We can see the same kind of thinking in the prologue to the Wyclif Bible: "But alas! alas! where king Jozophat sente his princis, and dekenes, and prestis, to ech citee of his rewme with the book of Goddis lawe, to techen opinly Goddis lawe to the puple, summe cristene lordis senden general lettris to alle her mynistris . . . that the pardouns of the bisschopis of Rome, that ben opin leesingis . . . be prechid generaly in her rewmes. . ." (I.29-30). How much, the sense is, could Christian leaders learn even from such a Jew, instead of which they act the way Jews are generally thought to act. Thus the "lewed vicory" expresses his desire that cardinals should confine themselves to "Avenon among Iewes" (XXI.422). Pearsall says that this refers to Jewish moneylenders at Avignon (358), but in the Good Parliament "Two great bills of petitions sent forward by the commons grumbled bitterly at all the old abuses under which the national church continued to suffer . . . never had the language of complaint been more violent against the traffic in benefices by those 'who dwell in the sinful city of Avignon,' against the exactions, the luxury and the corrupting influence of the papal agents or against the alien absentees, whose existence was more injurious to holy church than 'all the Jews and Saracens in the world'" (McFarlane 65-66). These corrupt churchmen, whose priestly ancestors were constant targets of the prophets, are worse than Jews. The "lewed vicory," in referring to the members of the papal court in Avignon as Jews, is making a prophetic comment on the corrupt nature of that court, tying together the biblical and contemporary worlds.[10]

Yet another connection between *Piers Plowman* and the prophets can be found in Langland's frequent references to plagues, hunger, and other natural disasters. We have already seen examples of prophetic threats against the people for not following God's teaching (e.g., Isaiah 1:20: "if you . . . will provoke me to wrath: the sword shall devour you") and there are numerous instances when disasters are explained as divine punishment. The most obvious example is the ten plagues, but there are others, such as the plague that befell the Israelites after their demand for meat (Numbers 11:33). To inhabitants of fourteenth-century England and survivors of the plague, such references had a particular relevance that Langland made use of. Thus Reason

> preuede þat this pestelences was for puyre synne
> And the south-weste wynde on a Saturday at euene
> Was pertliche for pruyde and for no poynt elles.
> (V.115-17)

Later we learn that pride is so common in England "That preyeres haen no power this pestilences to lette" (XI.60) and at the end of the poem we see Kynde defend the inhabitants of Unity by bringing the plague upon its attackers (XXII.80-105). In Passus VIII, Hunger descends on the society as a punishment for the lack of cooperation among its members and for the general level of corruption that Piers sees there. Langland uses these natural disasters just as the prophets did. Although this theme may have been a commonplace, it is yet one more indication of Langland's reliance on the prophets in developing his own prophetic stance.

These references to disasters are clearly common to Langland and the prophets. There is another connection between them that is somewhat less obvious and harder to demonstrate. Anne Middleton refers to this connection when she discusses the problem of explaining what happens in *Piers Plowman*: "Attempts to recount the whole narration of this journey as a developing succession of acts and events tend to emphasize discontinuity rather than progression. It is not quite a story, nor a collection of shorter ones" (1982, 92). Other readers have felt the same way. Muscatine, for example, says that "Langland's space is surrealistic . . . artistic logic fades as one scene reels and melts into the next, as characters . . . appear and disappear or are forgotten. . . . And so the poem goes, existing in no one realm of space and location, invoking successive spatial images for limited and temporary effect without tending to the relations between them" (88-9). This discontinuity and cavalier treatment of space and time can also be explained by Langland's use of the prophetic texts.

Erich Auerbach, in his important essay "Odysseus' Scar," discusses the narrative technique used by the biblical authors in the story of Isaac's near sacrifice. As Auerbach points out, the story "unrolls with no episodes in a few independent sentences whose syntactical connection is of the most rudimentary form" (1957, 7). The reader has no idea when or where the story occurred, no idea of what Abraham and Isaac may have discussed on their three-day journey. There is in the story almost no concern for space and time. "The journey is like a silent progress through the indeterminate and the contingent . . . a process which has no present, which is inserted, like a blank duration, between what has passed and what lies ahead" (1957, 7). If this attitude toward space and time is present in a story with a clear narrative structure, how much more is it a factor in the prophetic texts, which sometimes have a rudimentary narrative structure but which are not narratives.[11] We may know the historical background of the prophecies, but we frequently cannot relate one chapter to another. This discontinuity is the result of the piecemeal composition (or redaction) of the prophetic texts as well as of the world view that we see throughout the Old Testament. As Auerbach explains, "As a composition, the Old Testament is incomparably less unified than the Homeric poems, it is more obviously pieced together — but the various components all belong to one concept of universal history and its interpretation" (1957, 14). We saw this thematic continuity earlier when we examined the imagery of Isaiah: the kind of thematic continuity that ran among those images runs also among the chapters of the prophets. Thus, in his commentary on Ezekiel 29, Jerome explains why prophecies from the tenth year and the twenty-seventh year are joined together by citing the importance of theme over chronology (414-15). Chronology is not terribly important because biblical texts exist essentially outside of time, against a background of eternity.

This attitude toward space and time in the biblical texts was reinforced by early and medieval exegesis. The Christian technique of reading the Old Testament by looking for types and prophecies of the New tended to blur the temporal distinctions between them. If, for example, Isaiah is seen as describing the life of Christ, the centuries that separate Isaiah and Christ become unimportant, and the same thing holds true if we project forward to the end of time. As Murtaugh says, "The Incarnation happens again, or it *still* happens in some way that transcends the very history it informs and makes 'again' meaningless" (29). The biblical stories happened not just once, but they continued to happen, as we see in Langland's retelling of the Passion. This is why it was so easy for later writers to see their own times in terms of biblical times. Thus, in describing fourteenth-century corruption, the prologue to the Wyclif Bible says, "now Manasses settith idolis opinly in the temple of God, and sterith men gretly to do idolatrie, and cherischen hem that breken opinly Goddis heestis, and punysche hem soore, as hethene men either eretikes, that bisien hem to lerne, kepe, and teche Goddis heestis. . . . Therfore, as Mychee the prophete seith in iij. c., thei hyilden pore men, and eten her flesch . . ." (I.33-34). It is not simply that the rulers are like Manasses. Manasses himself is still operating, still behaving in the ways described by Micah, who, significantly, did not prophesy at the time of Manasses, but for whom that wicked king was still seen as a living presence.

Langland has Conscience provide another explicit example:

> "I, Consience, knowe this, for Kynde Wit me tauhte,
> That resoun shal regne and reumes gouerne
> And riht as Agag hadde happe shal somme;
> Samuel shal sle hym and Sauel shal be yblamed
> And David shal be ydyademed and adaunte alle oure
>   enemyes
> And o cristene kyng kepe vs echone."

> (III.436-41)

This is not a prophecy of what the audience knew had happened already. It is, rather, a restatement of the pattern that will be followed again and lead to the establishment of a king in the mold of David.

Furthermore, such patterns can be kept in mind as a totality: "Preie we to God with al our herte, that sithen lordis and prelatis suen Manasses in these opyn synnes, God stire hem to sue Manasses in very penaunce" (Wyclif Bible I.34). If Manasses is the controlling spirit of the age, perhaps his pattern of ultimate repentance will be carried through to its end.

Similarly, words that are used in one part of the Bible are read in the context of their use elsewhere in the Bible. Jerome uses this technique constantly. For example, in commenting on Ezekiel 2:8, "open thy mouth," Jerome recalls Psalm 80:11 ("open thy mouth wide"), Psalm 118:131 ("I opened my mouth"), and II Corinthians 6:11 ("Our mouth is open to you"). After all, if the Bible is the inspired word of God, then all the words in the Bible, regardless of how far apart they are temporally or spatially, are related, and their immediate historical background is not terribly important. What is important are the resonances, the relationships, the discovery of patterns, all of which contribute, for the Christian exegete, to the single overarching message of salvation. This kind of exegesis, in combination with the sometimes jumbled nature of the biblical texts, con- tributes to what we might consider a discontinuous view of the Bible, though to a medieval reader such verbal and thematic acrobatics might well have indicated a higher level of continuity and unity than our modern view of the Bible would allow.

It should come as no surprise, then, that if *Piers Plowman* was composed under the inspiration of the prophets, it shares their disjunctive style. In our earlier examination of the imagery in Isaiah 1:4-8, we saw how Isaiah piled on and shifted his imagery to make his points more effectively, and anyone who has gotten lost in a passage of *Piers Plowman* will recognize that Langland did much the same thing. We can also see his disjunctiveness in the larger structure of the poem. *Piers Plowman* is not a narrative with a plot that begins at one temporal spot and ends at another, though there are enough narrative episodes to give that impression, as there are, to various degrees, in the prophets. But overall *Piers Plowman* is a series of visions, related thematically, with a multitude of verbal echoes. Spatially it is largely indeterminate, though it includes scenes in various English sites and in Jerusalem. Temporally, it jumps around through fourteen centuries. Nonetheless, Langland's themes and words unify this ap- parent disorder, as indeed does his use of biblical quotations. Not only do they, as John Alford has shown, provide a structure to the poem, being "related to each other *horizontally* . . . and to the English portions of the poem *vertically*" (1977, 96),[12] but they reflect an idea of unity that can be seen in Jerome's attempts to find biblical authors quoting each other. (In addition, of course, that multitude of biblical quotations gives a kind of divine sanction to Langland's words, providing a firm foundation for his prophetic stance.)

Similarly, Langland's characters and visions seem to fade in and out like those of the prophets. The suffering servant in Isaiah, for example, seems to appear almost arbitrarily (much like Piers himself) over the span of several chapters; or Ezekiel, in chapter 37, can combine two separate visions, that of the valley of dry bones and that of the allegorical joining together of two sticks to represent Judah and Israel. When these visions occurred we are not told, but their thematic relationship — the resurrection of a dead nation and the joining together of the parts of that nation — show that they are obviously related. In

Piers Plowman, characters seem to appear out of nowhere (a good example is Trajan) and scenes form with no immediately apparent relationship to what comes before or after, although the unity of the poem is never jeopardized. These peculiar ways of treating space and time constitute yet another link between Langland's poem and his prophetic sources.[13]

So, too, does Will's picture of himself. What he wears has important thematic overtones, whether he is "yclothed as a lollare" (V.2) or "Wollewaerd and watschoed" (XX.1), dressed as a mendicant (XV.3) or dressed "derely" (XXI.2). Isaiah makes one of his strongest points by going barefoot and naked (20) and Jeremiah makes a symbol out of his linen girdle (13:1-7) and the chains that he wears (27-28), just as later bearers of divine messages, like St. Francis, distinguished themselves with symbolic clothing and actions. Will's description of himself as a shepherd at the poem's very beginning recalls Amos, "who was among the herdsmen of Thecua" (1:1). Will's humility,[14] as in the conclusion of the autobiographical passage in Passus V or in his relating to us Holy Church's reference to him as "thow dotede daffe" (I.138), his occasional references to his family, his rejection by his Cornhill associates, his picture of himself growing old and suffering in the process of his attempt to understand — all recall bits of autobiography that can be found in the prophets; and though they may be tangential, they fit in with the prophetic pattern that we have been observing.

There are also a great many passages in the poem that simply sound prophetic. These are passages in which either the narrator or one of Will's interlocutors launches into a prophetic denunciation of the uncaring rich, of the hypocritical clergy, or of wicked rulers, often threatening them specifically or the community as a whole with punishment:

> Many sondry sorwes in citees falleth ofte,
> Bothe thorw fuyr and thorw flood, al thorw fals peple
> That bygyleth goode men and greueth hem wrongly,
> The whiche þat crien on here knees þat Crist hem
>   auenge . . .
> And thenne falleth ther fuyr on fals men houses
> And goode mennes for her gultes gloweth on fuyr aftur.
>   (III.90-103)

Such condemnations of all who oppress the righteous can be found everywhere in the prophets, as can promises of punishment that will afflict everyone in the community, the righteous as well as the unrighteous. Isaiah announces, "Behold the Lord shall lay waste the earth, and shall strip it, and shall afflict the face thereof, and scatter abroad the inhabitants thereof. And it shall be as with the people, so with the priest: and as with the servant, so with his master: as with the handmaid, so with her mistress: as with the buyer, so with the seller: as with the lender, so with the borrower: as with him that calleth for his money, so with him that oweth" (24:1-2). On a more positive note, we read in *Piers Plowman*:

> Ac he þat speneth his speche and speketh for þe pore
> That innocent and nedy is and no man harm wolde,
> That conforteth suche in eny caes and coueyteth nat here
>   3iftes
> And for þe loue of oure lord lawe for hem declareth
> Shal haue grace of a good ende and greet ioye aftur.
>   (IX.46-50)

This passage is like many in the prophets in which the good are praised, such as the concluding verse of Hosea: "Who is wise, and he shall understand these things? prudent, and he shall know these things? for the ways of the Lord are right, and the just shall walk in them: but the transgressors shall fall in them" (Hosea 14:10). The concluding contrast between the just and the transgressors, so common in the prophets, recalls the next lines in Passus IX, which begin "Beth ywar," and which constitute a stern warning to the unrighteous. It would be easy — and tiresome — to multiply examples of such prophetic speech in *Piers Plowman*. No doubt such passages gave inspiration to the rebels in 1381. No doubt they also have contributed to the vague feeling shared by so many of Langland's readers that this poem is somehow prophetic. Langland's constant return to the necessity of caring for the poor — "y rede 3ow riche, haueth reuthe vppon pe pore" (I.171) — is enough to bring the prophets to mind. And these are also among the passages that make the poem seem like a sermon.

Finally, although predicting the future was not the prophets' main task, there are certainly what appear to be predictive passages in their works, as there seem to be in *Piers Plowman*. One of Langland's best examples, which we glanced at earlier, concludes Passus VIII:

> Ac y warne 3ow werkmen, wynneth whiles 3e mowe,
> For Hunger hiderwardes hasteth hym faste.
> He shal awake thorw water, wastors to chaste,
> And ar few 3eres be fulfeld famyne shal aryse,
> And so sayth Saturne and sente vs to warne.
> Thorw flodes and thorw foule wederes fruyttes shollen fayle;
> Pruyde and pestilences shal moche peple feche.
> Thre shypes and a schaef with an viii folwynge
> Shal brynge bane and batayle on bothe half þe mone.
> And thenne shal deth withdrawe and derthe be iustice
> And Dawe þe deluare dey for defaute
> But yf god of his goodnesse graunte vs a trewe.
>   (VIII.343-54)

Bloomfield focuses on what he considers the apocalyptic aspects of this and other prophecies (1961, 112 and 211-12), and admittedly they provide tempting riddles whose decipherment would be desirable. Nonetheless, these riddles are not of paramount importance. Far more important is the practical, prophetic message of this passage. When Will says this — and the Will who says it can hardly be classified as a "dotede daffe" — he has just seen the failure of the plowing of the half-acre and Hunger's attack on the people. The failure in plowing is the result of a larger societal failure, in which the various estates either neglect or are incapable of fulfilling their societal responsibilities. This divided and self-seeking society is doomed, and one natural consequence of their failure to plow is the advent of Hunger. At the end of the passus, just to be sure that no one has missed the point, Langland has Will summarize it and explain its current application. One of the functions of the coming famine is to chastise "wastors," and one of its consequences will be the onset of plague. Terrible times are at hand, because God is about to punish the people.

Still, this is not an outright prediction; there is hope: "So god gyueth nothyng þat *si* ne is the glose" (III.328). All that Will predicts here will come true "But yf god of his goodnesse graunte vs a trewe." "Trewe" means "truce", of course, or possibly "covenant," but it is related to "trust," so that the line implies that famine and plague can be forestalled if God makes a truce with us by giving us trust, by endowing us with a will to function together, as a society, for the common profit, thereby serving God. The people can either learn that lesson now from Will's words or learn it later, after suffering. This is much the same pattern that we find in Isaiah 24-27.[15] In Isaiah 24 we read, "1. Behold the Lord shall lay waste the earth, and shall strip it, and shall afflict the face thereof, and scatter abroad the inhabitants thereof. 2. And it shall be as with the people, so with the priest: and as with the servant, so with the master . . . as with the buyer, so with the seller. . . . 3. With desolation shall the earth be laid waste. . . . 5. And the earth is infected by the inhabitants thereof: because they have transgressed the laws, they have changed the ordinances, they have broken the everlasting covenant." This passage is related to the conclusion of Passus VIII in a number of ways. First, it is a prediction of coming disaster as punishment for the nation's evil behavior. Second, with its emphasis on the earth being laid waste, it implies the hunger, floods, and foul weather cited by Langland. And third, it mentions the "everlasting covenant" that corresponds to Langland's "trewe." If the prophet's task is indeed to encourage the people to repent, Isaiah's reference to the broken covenant is a reminder that the covenant can be repaired. This is at least part of the import of Isaiah 25-27, chapters that not only contain a great deal of possibly apocalyptic imagery but that show how good things can be when the covenant is restored.

It can hardly be a coincidence, therefore, that Langland's Passus IX concerns Truth's Pardon, a pardon heavily dependent on the prophetic conditions.[16] Passus IX begins

> Treuthe herde telle her-of and to Peres sente
> To taken his teme and tilion þe erthe,
> And purchasede hym a pardoun *a pena et a culpa*,
> For hym and his ayres for euere to ben assoiled,
> And bad hym holden hym at hoem and eryen his leyes
> And alle þat holpe hym to erye, to sette or to sowe
> Or eny manere mester þat myhte Peres auayle,
> Pardoun with Peres þe plouhman perpetuelly he graunteth.
>   (IX.1-8)

What has Truth heard tell of? Apparently Truth has heard about the actions of Passus VIII and of the warning that concludes that Passus and has therefore sent the pardon, which, when we finally hear its terms, is a simple statement of the "trewe" that Will mentions at the end of Passus VIII: if you do well, "god shal haue thy soule" (IX.291); and if you do evil, you shall "haue euele" (IX.292). This, of course, returns us to Isaiah 1, "cease to do perversely, learn to do well," and sets the stage for Will's attempts at clarifying what it means to do well in the second half of the poem.

There is yet another point to be made here. Why is this pardon sent to a plowman? In Isaiah 28 we find: "24. Shall the ploughman plough all the day to sow, shall he open and harrow his ground? 25. Will he not, when he hath made plain the surface thereof, sow gith, and scatter cumin, and put wheat in order, and barley, and millet. . . ? 26. For he will instruct him in judgment: his God will teach him." To make the relationship to IX.6 more obvious, here is Isaiah 28:24-5 in the Wyclif translation: "Whether al day shal ere the erere, that he sowe, and forth kutten, and purge his erthe? Whether not, when he shal euenen therto his face, he shal sowe the sed gith, and the comyn sprengen, and sette the whete bi order. . ?" (III.273). The picture of the plowman, whose job is "to erye, to sette or to sowe," being instructed about the Pardon by God depends at least in part on Isaiah, as does this whole episode from the end of Passus VIII through Passus IX. Furthermore, Elizabeth Kirk, in a detailed study of the plowman figure, illustrates the ways in which the plowman unites economic, political, and religious matters (1988, 15).

Returning, then, to the prediction at the conclusion of Passus VIII, we can see that it really is not the kind of prediction that it seemed to be. It is a prophetic warning of what can happen *if* the people persist in their evil ways. It is an example of forthtelling rather than foretelling, of Langland reading the present and showing the potential consequences of the present, just as the biblical prophets did. In other apparently predictive passages (III.436-81; IV.92-132; and V.168-79), the same principles hold true, except that these passages also contain more definite promises of better times to come:

> Ac þer shal come a kyng and confesse ʒow alle
> And bete ʒow, as þe bible telleth, for brekynge of ʒoure
>   reule
> And amende ʒowe monkes, bothe moniales and chanons,
> And potte ʒowe to ʒoure penaunce, *Ad pristinum statum ire*,
> And barones and here barnes blame ʒow and repreue . . .
> Freres in here fraytour shal fynde þat tyme
> Bred withouten beggynge to lyue by euere aftur . . .
>   (V.168-74)

Such passages, with their promise of both punishment and reconciliation, have many counterparts in the prophets. Isaiah frequently tells the people that because of their sins they must be purged or purified, after which they will live in a proper relationship with God: "And I will turn my hand to thee, and I will clean purge away thy dross, and I will take away all thy tin. And I will restore thy judges as they were before . . ." (1:25-6). All of the allegedly predictive passages in *Piers Plowman* are like the allegedly predictive passages in the prophets and remind us that in both cases "the prophet's role was not to predict but to reform" (Emmerson 46).

It should now be clear how deeply indebted Langland was to the prophets, especially Isaiah. Isaiah's abundant Christology, his use of allegorical names, his personifications (or at least a medieval perception of his personifications), his treatment of space and time, his imagery, as well as his constant insistence on the need for doing well, for the establishment of proper behavior in society, all appear in *Piers Plowman*. In addition, Langland's frequent references to the Jews, his use of lines from the prophet, his comments on various pestilences, and his extensive use of Isaiah 1 − all of these indicate the extent of Langland's reliance on the prophet for inspiration. Of course, many of these elements Langland could have found elsewhere. Many were commonplaces and were generally available, and it would be a simple task to list all of their possible sources, but the only place he could have found them all together is in the prophets. Such circumstantial evidence would thus point to the prophets as a major source of Langland's approach to his poem. Sensing himself in an historical and moral situation akin to that described in Kings,[17] Langland addressed the problems as the biblical prophets had, at least in his fourteenth-century understanding of the prophets. After all, if the problems were the same, so were the solutions, especially in light of the typological approach to the Bible. In short, *Piers Plowman* is a fourteenth-century attempt to address current problems in the eternally valid terms of the prophets. In that sense it is a conscious imitation of biblical prophecy.

If this is the case, we need not be surprised at the kind of works with which *Piers Plowman* was generally associated. Anne Middleton, in studying the works with which *Piers Plowman* manuscripts were bound, discovered that "The two kinds of content most often found with it are religious instruction and historical narration" (1982a, 104). These two kinds of content are perfectly combined in both the prophets and in *Piers Plowman*, and it would seem that the medieval scribes had a good idea of the type of work they were dealing with. It now remains for us to consider the implications of this aspect of Langland's work for an understanding of *Piers Plowman*.

V. *Piers Plowman* and Prophecy

Langland's use of the prophets is more than a curiosity or even a structural device. In fact his use of the prophets has important implications for our understanding of the poem, both by clarifying some of its controversial aspects and by casting new light on other aspects. This is most emphatically not to say that the recognition of Langland's prophetic stance is meant to displace other readings of the poem. In fact it will often give added support to other readings by providing a background against which they can be set. It is essential to remember in what follows, however, that Langland, like the prophets, was not a theologian. He was not overly concerned with the fine points of doctrine. He was concerned with the inappropriate behavior of the English people and their secular and religious leaders. And, like the prophets, he was moved to address these concerns. His message is recognition and reform, not the enunciation or investigation of doctrine.

Still, we must acknowledge that medieval commentators often did view the prophets as conveyers of theological doctrine, and to some extent this is the picture of the prophets that Langland would have inherited. On the other hand, in the fourteenth century there was "a marked reaction against the excessive intellectualism and excessive subtlety of scholasticism. This represents a very old tradition, going back in some form to those Fathers, such as St. Ambrose, who were fond of contrasting Gospel simplicity with sophisticated pagan philosophy; God had revealed Himself to fishermen, not philosophers" (Pantin 132). This tradition received support from the increasing focus on the literal level of the Bible in the late Middle Ages and can be seen in the writings of Wyclif, for instance. Langland's method, like Wyclif's, was, as much as possible, to return to the biblical text. This was undoubtedly among the reasons for Langland's popularity in the English Reformation and for the various attempts to see him as a precursor or predictor of the Reformation. We must be careful, therefore, not to make a scholastic out of him. As Conscience tells the friars, "ʒow shal no thyng lakke/With þat ʒe leve logyk and lerneth for to louye"

(XXII.249-50). Instead we must try to understand his view of the problems that beset his society and look at his solutions to those problems.

1. THE END OF THE POEM

It may be best, strangely enough, to begin with the poem's last two passus. It is hard to believe that these passus, as they stand in the C-Text, are what Langland intended. After his revisions throughout the rest of the poem, surely he intended to revise these as well. Still, since conjecture on why he did not would be fruitless, we have no choice but to deal with them as they are.

The conclusion of *Piers Plowman* is often taken to be largely apocalyptic. Emmerson, after drawing a clear distinction between the prophetic and the apocalyptic, says, "In the poem's concluding passus, Langland portrays the world suffering from the evils of the last days. After listening to a long harangue by Need, Will ... is shown an apocalyptic vision of the imminent future — the attack of Antichrist upon Unity" (53). I would prefer a different interpretation: The last two passus illustrate Langland's view of his own day, of the failures of his own day, with apocalyptic overtones.

Langland prepares us for this view at the end of Passus XX, when the Four Daughters of God have been reconciled. First

> Treuth trompede tho and song *Te deum laudamus*,
> And thenne lutede Loue in a loude note,
> *Ecce quam bonum et quam jocundum est, etc.* . . . .
> (XX.468-69)

That "etc." is important, for in Psalm 133, the whole first verse reads, as we saw in Chapter III, "Ecce quam bonum et quam iucundum/Habitare fratres in unum." The translation of this verse in the Douay Bible is, while not literally accurate, significant in relation to Langland: "Behold how good and how pleasant it is for brethren to dwell together in unity." The psalmist's "in unum" means only "together," but it seems certain that Langland, with an allegorical outlook, treated the verse as the translators did, reading "in unum" not just as "together" but also as "in unity," or, more precisely, "in Unity." This Unity, "Holy Chirche an Englisch" (XXI.329), is the place where brothers should dwell together, and how good and how pleasant that would be Langland shows us in Passus XXI. Langland had hinted at this development early in the poem, in his famous grammatical explanation of "mede" and "mercede":

> Ac adiectyf and sustantyf is as y her tolde,
> That is unite acordaunde in case, in gendre and in noumbre,
> And is to mene in oure mouth more no mynne
> But þat alle maner men, wymmen and childrene
> Sholde confourme hem to o kynde on holy kyrke to bileue
> And coueyte þe case when thei couthe vunderstande
> To syke for here synnes and soffre harde penaunces
> For þat lordes loue that for oure loue deyede
> And coueytede our kynde and be kald in oure name,
> *Deus homo,*
> And nyme hym into our noumbre now and euermore.
>
> (III.393-402)

Here unity in case, gender, and number is associated with unity in a single church, with repentance, and with the Crucifixion. Similarly, the building of Unity in Passus XXI follows the Crucifixion and represents the establishment of Holy Church. So, too, the troubles that beset Unity in Passus XXII are hinted at when Conscience and Reason tell the king to love "his comune" and remind him that "in heuene an heyh was an holy comune" until Lucifer rebelled (V.180-88). Reason concludes

> "Holde 30w in vnite, and he þat oþer wolde
> Is cause of alle combraunces to confounde a reume. . ."
>
> (V.189-90)

This recalls Liberum Arbitrium's definition of Holy Church:

> "Lief and loue and leutee in o byleue and lawe,
> A loue-knotte of leutee and of lele byleue,
> Alle kyne cristene cleuynge on o will,
> Withoute gyle and gabbyng gyue and sulle and lene."
>
> (XVII.126-29)

All of these passages point to the poem's end not precisely as a description of Apocalypse but as a description of the collapse of Holy Church as the result of the society's failure to maintain unity. Such a description necessarily contains apocalyptic elements, but we must remember that Langland's goal is the reform of society, not a description or a prediction of its end. If he were really apocalyptic, he might urge his readers to pray (and perhaps take shelter), but his focus is always on reform. The loosing of Antichrist, for example, is unarguably apocalyptic, but it does not mean that apocalypse is imminent. What is more important, or of more immediate concern for Langland, is that society has become divided — unity is gone. Members of the good society should without guile or lies, give, sell, and lend to others at least the three necessities, food, clothing, and drink, about which Holy Church had told Will in I.23-24. But in Passus XXII, Need attacks the society, and instead of responding as a "comune," the society responds with selfishness, so that Need's advice finally is to take those necessities. Because the society, living in Unity, should provide for each of its members, Need's advice represents the collapse of unity into selfishness, a collapse that is shown in detail through the rest of the passus.[1] The poem concludes with Conscience's pilgrimage to find Piers, who can restore the unity to Unity. Langland has traced the history of the Church down to his own time, and the poem's conclusion offers a realistic picture of the Church in collapse but capable of reconstruction.[2]

Despite the mentions of Antichrist, then, Langland does not develop the apocalyptic imagery that he might have in the poem's concluding passus. These passus are, rather, a summary repetition of much that has come before, indicating the possibility of a just human society and the reasons that such a society does not exist, which naturally are associated with the Antichrist. If Langland were indeed adopting an apocalyptic stance here, his emphasis on individual and societal repentance might be out of place. These passus are similar to many chapters in the prophets in which the prophets castigate the people for their sins while holding out the possibility that repentance and good behavior will restore the society to its ideal state. That such a restoration is possible we can see from the earlier episode involving Piers and Hunger. In Passus VIII, when the society breaks down, when people stop doing their jobs, the natural consequence is the arrival of Hunger. As a result

> Tho were faytours afered and flowen into Peres bernes
> And flapton on with flales fro morwen til euen,
> That Hunger was nat hardy on hem for to loke.
> For a potte ful of potage þat Peres wyf made
> An heep of eremytes henten hem spades,
> Sputeden and spradden donge in dispit of Hunger.
> (VIII.179-84)

Because of Hunger, even the "faytours" and "eremytes," not to mention the "freres" (191) enter Piers's barn, are fed, and do their assigned chores. The problem, of course, as both Langland and the prophets recognize, is that this situation is temporary. As soon as conditions improve, as soon as Hunger has disappeared, the old selfishness will return. The same kind of scene recurs in Passus XXII when Kynde sends the plague, then calls it off to see whether the people would

> Leue pruyde priueyliche and be parfyt cristene.
> And Kynde sesede tho, to se þe peple amende.
>
> (XXII.108-9)

Unfortunately, this time the people do not amend. The plague has been ineffective. This was precisely the situation when Langland was writing *Piers Plowman*. Even after the devastating series of plagues in the fourteenth century, the English persisted in their wickedness. Hence Unity collapsed and hence Langland felt compelled to produce his poem in an attempt to make his society reform and to restore Unity. Conscience — and there is nothing to indicate that this is one individual's conscience — must try to find Piers so that this dream will again become a reality, as it was in the early days of Christianity described in Passus XXI, so that the Church will function as it should.

In our discussion of the concluding passus, we have been focusing on the religious aspect, which is only natural, since we are told that Unity is Holy Church. Nonetheless, the religious aspect is not the only important one. The Church by itself cannot supply Unity. Anna Baldwin says, "In spite of his earlier suggestions for political reform, Langland ends the poem with a plea for moral reform" (56) and she adds, "It would seem then that, like most 'political' poets of the time, Langland does not separate the political from the moral" (81). As we saw in examining the prophets, they did not make a distinction among the political, the religious, and the moral realms. Rather they emphasized the interrelationships, the interdependence, among those realms. No one of them can function properly without the others. This motif was central to Langland's thought.

2. THE UNITY OF UNITY

Many critics of *Piers Plowman* have maintained that Langland was primarily interested in individual salvation. Vasta, for example, says, "The subject of *Piers Plowman*... is not man in society, or the reform of society that cannot be brought about unless each individual reforms; it is personal salvation purely and simply" (33). Such a view surely oversimplifies Langland's thought and, in fact, falls into the very trap about which Langland warned. Langland was certainly concerned with personal salvation, but, like the prophets, he recognized the communal nature of earthly human existence and the interdependence of personal and communal life. The subject, of course, is complex, but Langland's continued attention to societal failures, like the prophets' denunciations of entire peoples, makes it clear that his concerns transcended the selfishness of a total focus on individual salvation. What Anne Hudson said about Wyclif's thought could apply equally well to Langland's: "All forms of 'private religion,' that is any way of life, monastic, fraternal, or anchoritic, that removed the individual from normal society ... together with prayers for the dead, indulgences, worship of images, pilgrimages, and the sale of any sacraments, should be abolished" (251). We have already seen Langland comment negatively on prayers for the dead in Will's "call to prophecy." Like Wyclif, he also attacks "private religion," whether it be monastic or fraternal life or a concern for individual salvation that ignores communal needs. Following the example of Jeremiah, who was taken to Egypt, or of Ezekiel, who accompanied the exiles to Babylon, the individual cannot seek salvation separate from the community. Whether or not this doctrine was heretical is not relevant. It is the doctrine that Langland conveyed, based on his understanding of the prophets and the contemporary situation.[3]

Langland's frequent use of the words "comune" and "comune profit" is itself evidence of his concern, and his focus on such points as love and charity illustrates his meaning. We must remember that through most of the poem, Langland is exploring what it means to "do well"; and in keeping with Isaiah's examples of doing well, Langland's exploration largely concerns social activities. We can see this first in a negative example provided by Conscience:

> Ac þe moste partie of peple now puyr indirect semeth,
> For they wilnen and wolden as beste were for hemsulue
> Thow the kyng and þe comune al the coest hadde.
> Such inparfit peple repreueth alle resoun
> And halt hem vnstedefast for hem lakketh case.
>
> (III.382-86)

Such people, with their selfish concerns, their lack of care for the "comune," violate the dictates of reason, for it is reasonable that a society should work together for the "comune profit." Furthermore there is a religious dimension to the argument, as Langland shows in the next lines when he defines "unite" as the conforming of all people "to o kynde on holy kyrke to bileue" (III.397). Those who are selfish prevent, by definition, the establishment of Unity.

But we also see positive, perhaps ideal, examples of people working for the common profit. In the Prologue, in a passage reminiscent of Genesis 4:20-22, Langland seems to describe the origins of society, in what appears to have been a golden age:

> And thenne cam Kynde Wytt and clerkus he made
> And Conscience and Kynde Wit and knyghthed togedres
> Caste þat þe comunes sholde here comunes fynde.
> Kynde Wytt and þe comune contreued alle craftes
> And for most profitable a plogh gonne þei make,

With lele labour to lyue while lif on londe lasteth.

(Prol.141-46)

By "comune profit" Langland certainly does not mean the levelling of social classes. What he desires is the proper functioning of each class so that all may profit. Clerks and knights must work together with the people so that "þe comunes" can find "here comunes," both their provisions and the "common-ness," that which, like their need for provisions, they all share. Working together, they are able to make a plow that will benefit them all, if they continue to work together, for as long as there is life on earth. This last phrase is particularly important, for it highlights Langland's focus on earthly human life. It is not that he shares Montaigne's "*nonchalance de salut.*" It is simply that, like the prophets, he is dealing with problems of human existence. By working together, the society will be able to survive. This is what Reason tells Will in the call to prophecy, and Will's understanding of this point leads him to write the poem.

Langland provides us with a number of examples of societies that either work or do not, depending on how much the people care about "comune profit." Unfortunately those that work seem largely hypothetical, like Reason's descrip-tion of the kind of society in which he might find it possible to be merciful:

"Rede me nat," quod Resoun, "no reuthe to haue
Til lordes and ladies louen alle treuthe. . .
Til clerkene coueytise be cloth for þe pore. . .
Til þat lerede men lyue as thei lere and teche
And til þe kynges consayl be alle comune profit
And til byschopes ben bakeres, breweres and taylours. . .

(IV.108-20)

Here again we see different classes — lords, clerks, scholars, kings, and bishops — working together. In such a society Reason would be able to show pity, but present society is nothing like that. Like the societies addressed by the prophets, it has not earned the right to pity. Furthermore, the problem lies not with any single class. If some of them worked properly, the others would be better as well:

3if knyhthoed and kynde wit and þe comune and consience
Togederes louyen lelelyche, leueth hit, bisshopes,
The lordschipe of londes lese 3e shal for euer
And lyuen as *Leuitici* dede and as our lord 3ow techeth. . . .

(XVII.216-19)

Over and over Langland presents us with pictures of society as it should run (often, as in the above passage, based on an Old Testament model), for the "comune profit," and then contrasts that ideal with the way society actually runs. There is no sense of development in these pictures, just as there is no development in the prophets. The poet is simply finding new ways to illustrate his point, that all the facets of society must work together justly in order for that society to continue, thereby making possible both individual and communal salvation.

This point is made quite clearly in the poem's most detailed picture of societal collapse aside from the fall of Unity, the plowing of the half-acre, which Spearing describes as "a further allegory of the attempt to set up a just society, now seen not as an end in itself but as a means to salvation" (143). In this episode, everyone is given a task, and we can clearly see the interdependence of the classes when the knight apologizes for not being able to plow and Piers explains that he will plow for them both if the knight will protect him and the church:

> In couenant þat thow kepe holy kerke and mysulue
> Fro wastores and fro wikked men þat þis world struyen. . .
>
> (VIII.26-27)

The use of the word "covenant" here, foreshadowing the "trewe" mentioned at the end of the passus, reinforces the sacred nature of these societal bonds. Over and over Langland makes this point and shows the evil consequences of the breakdown of the covenant. Frequently the breakdown is caused by the clergy or by the rulers, who are natural targets of such criticism, but in Passus VIII the breakdown comes from the lower classes, the shirkers, as a result of whose inaction Hunger attacks the whole society. While the lower classes have often escaped Langland's castigation, this criticism is especially sharp. It is not only one part of the society that is corrupt. As Isaiah says, "From the sole of the foot unto the top of the head, there is no soundness therein" (1:6). Like Isaiah, Langland spares no one from his criticism. Furthermore, this episode illustrates the relationship among the political, moral, and religious realms in another way. If we keep in mind that the overall narrative of *Piers Plowman* is minimal, we can see that the story of Unity is not so much a development of this episode as it is a recapitulation, in other allegorical terms, of the collapse of society; but whereas the collapse in Passus VIII is described primarily in political terms, that at the poem's end is described primarily in religious terms. The two societal collapses are the same, but Langland explains them from two different though intertwined perspectives. If the political body were healthy, it could help to heal the religious body; and if the religious body were healthy, it could help to heal the political. But given the symbiotic relationship between them, when both are diseased, neither can be healed separately. Healing — or reform — must permeate the entire society.

As part of the healing process, Langland describes the ideal state of both political and religious institution. Like the prophets, who frequently describe the way things should be, without necessarily telling exactly how they can get that way (a common criticism, as we saw, of Wyclif's social program), Langland often provides us with pictures of the ideal. Thus, after Will asks Holy Church the poem's key question,

> "Teche me to no tresor, but telle me this ilke,
> How Y may saue my soule, þat saynt art yholde"
>
> (I.79-80)

Holy Church first tells him to be "trewe of tonge" and to do good works, but she then tells him the function of clerks (to which we shall return) and then of kings:

> "Kynges and knyghtes sholde kepen hit by resoun
> Rydon and rappe adoun in reumes aboute
> And take *transgressores* and teyen hem faste
> Til Treuthe hadde termyned here trespas to þe ende,
> And halden with hem and here þat han trewe accion
> And for no lordene loue leue þe trewe partie."
>
> (I.90-95)

The function of the ruling class is to defend Truth, which is, as Pearsall says (47), divine law. This may be a medieval commonplace, but it is no less true for that; and Langland would have found this function described many times in the prophets. We need only think of their frequent addresses directed specifically to the kings. Langland goes on to emphasize the relationship between the political and religious realms by citing David's dubbing of knights and then God's dubbing of the angels as "knights." The earthly king, with his biblical and heavenly counterparts, is as responsible for the safety and salvation of his people as are the religious leaders.

This notion, of course, is the ideal. The reality is somewhat different, as the Meed episode illustrates and as Langland shows again later:

> And thenne cam þer a kyng and bi his corone saide:
> "Y am kyng with croune the comune to reule
> And holy kyrke and clerge fro cursed men to defende.
> And yf me lakketh to lyue by, þe lawe wol þat y take hit
> Ther y may hastilokest hit haue, for y am heed of lawe
> And 3e ben bote membres and y aboue alle."
>
> (XXI.465-70)

Here the king gives passing recognition to his duties, but his real thoughts are on his ability to take what he needs. His assertion that "ȝe ben bote membres" hardly lives up to Reason's claim that "þe comune is the kynges tresor" (V.181); and Conscience's response to the king emphasizes the ruler's duties rather than his rights:

> "In condicioun," quod Consience, "þat þou þe comune
>   defende
> And rewle thy rewme in resoun riht wel and in treuthe,
> Than haue thow al thyn askyng as thy lawe asketh."
>
> (XXI.477-79)

Of course, immediately after this exchange Unity is attacked and the king makes no effort to save it, thereby demonstrating the emptiness of his earlier claim. It is as Isaiah says: "The princes are faithless . . . they run after rewards." In the light of such concerns, Langland's alleged focus on individual salvation would be selfish and out of place. His concern is with the whole of society, the "comune profit."

This attitude can be seen as well in Langland's attacks on religious institutions. After telling Will how to achieve salvation, Holy Church explains the function of clerks:

> "Clerkes þat knowen hit is thus sholde kenne it aboute,
> For cristene and vncristene claymeth it echone."
>
> (I.88-89)

Their job is to teach about Truth. Exactly what that teaching entails will be examined later; but it is clear that whatever it means, the clerks have not been doing it, with consequences that are evident in the long Latin quotation following XVI.271, which shows corruption spreading from the Church to both individuals and the nation. Because Langland's attitude toward contemporary religious observance, the apparent emphasis on external show rather than internal devotion, is well known, we need not multiply examples. His feelings can be understood simply by examining the phenomenon of pilgrimage.

Langland's complaint about pilgrimages is that they are hollow religious gestures. They are an external show of religiosity that lacks all substance. Thus, after the confessions of the sins, thousands of men clamor to go on a pilgrimage to Truth. Just as the sins's repentance must be hollow — Sloth, for instance, will always be Sloth — so is the idea of the pilgrimage. Thus, they are all excited to go to Truth, "Ac þer ne was wye non so wys þat the way thither couthe" (VII.158), and even the well-travelled pilgrim admits that he has never heard of a pilgrim seeking Truth. Langland is here giving body to the numerous prophetic statements that reject empty ritual, typified by Isaiah's "Offer sacrifice no more in vain . . . for your hands are full of blood." Sightseeing tours dressed up like religious pilgrimages may be enjoyable, but they are an abomination. True pilgrimage is defined by Reason in his speech about the proper time to show pity:

> "And til saynt James be souhte there pore sykke lyggen,
> In prisones and in pore cotes be pilgrimages to Rome. . . "
>
> (IV.122-23)

If traditional pilgrimages are an empty show, true pilgrimages, not to Rome or Compostella but to prisons and poorhouses, contribute to the "comune profit." Their benefit accrues not only to the individual but to the entire society, and while they do not seem to be overtly religious acts, they, and not the traditional pilgrimages, are the true expression of Christianity. As Will recognizes later, "So Dowel passeth pardoun and pilgrimages to Rome" (IX.325). Again, the political, moral, and religious realms are intimately bound together, as we see perhaps even more clearly when Piers appears to give directions for the pilgrimage to Truth. According to Piers, the way to Truth lies through the Ten Commandments and the Christian virtues, all of which are difficult and none of which can provide the sheer enjoyment of a trip to Rome, so that a number of aspiring pilgrims abandon him immediately. To reinforce his point, Langland follows Piers's instructions with the plowing scene, in which by subtle transformations the plowing actually becomes the pilgrimage. The point of these transformations is again prophetic. Just as the prophets' audiences had made the error of distinguishing between religious and secular realms — bringing sacrifices to God but mistreating each other or relying on the presence of the Temple to protect them regardless of their misdeeds — so, too, has Langland's audience. Pilgrimages they treat as a sacred activity, plowing as a secular one. By transforming the plowing into the pilgrimage, Langland shows the artificiality of that supposed distinction. Neither an individual nor a society can find salvation through external rituals. This is the import of Piers's advice:

> "And yf Grace graunte the to go in in this wyse
> Thow shalt se Treuthe sitte in thy sulue herte,
> And solace thy soule and saue the fram payne
> And charge Charite a churche to make
> In thyne hole herte, to herborwe alle trewe
> And fynde alle manere folke fode to here soules . . . "
>
> (VII.254-59)

Pearsall notes here that the "journey to Truth ends in self-discovery, in the recognition of the spirit of Truth that dwells within" (142). However, it is essential to see here that the journey to Truth does not end in self-discovery.

Rather, self-discovery is the step next to the end of the journey, for the end of the journey to Truth is action. The person who sees Truth in his or her heart must then be moved to make that heart into a church and to find food for other people's souls. In this food image, Langland ties together the religious image of the pilgrimage, the secular image of plowing, and the social necessity of moral activity. They are, in essence, all the same, which is exactly the point that the prophets make so frequently. All of these realms stand in identical relationships to the "comune profit." They are merely different perspectives on the same subject.

Langland's attitude toward pilgrimages is like his attitude toward all external religious practices. Like the prophets, he is suspicious of them. This is why Conscience responds to Will's boasting about his prayers and penances, "By Crist, y can nat se this lyeth" (V.89). Langland's rejection of the "power of prayer" may well violate every commonplace about prayer, but we would be wrong to find ways to make him seem more orthodox. His rejection of prayer by itself as an effective response to the problems of his time is no different from the prophetic denigration of empty ritual, as we can see in several important passages. For example, in the plowing scene, as we saw earlier, Piers is told by the "faytours" who claim they cannot work,

> "And we praye for you, Peres, and for ȝoure plouh bothe
> That god for his grace ȝoure grayn multiplye
> And ȝelde ȝow of ȝoure almesse þat ȝe ȝeuen vs here."

Piers's response, recalling Will's comments about the "preyeres of a parfit man," is

> "ȝoure preyeres," quod Peres, "and ȝe parfyt weren,
> Myhte helpe. . . ."
>   (VIII.131-37)

However heartfelt their prayers might be — and they certainly should be sincere, since they are essentially prayers for food — those prayers by themselves are worthless. If the "faytours" were perfect, their prayers might be effective, but few human beings are perfect, and the rest of us must supplement our prayers with action. Langland makes this point even more forcefully in a passage that might have come straight from the prophets:

> Clerkes and knyhtes carpen of god ofte
> And haen muche in here mouth, ac mene in her herte.
> Freres and faytours haen founde vp suche questions
> To plese with proude men senes this pestelences,
> And prechyng at seynt Poules for puyr enuye of clerkes,
> That folk is nat ferme in þe faith ne fre of here godes

> Ne sory for here synnes; so ys pruyde enhanced
> In religion and in al þe reume amonges riche and pore
> That preyeres haen no power this pestilences to lette.
> For god is deef nowadayes and deyneth vs nat to here
> And gode men for oure gultes he al togrynt to deth.
> And ʒut this wreches of this world, is noen ywar by oþer,
> Ne for drede of eny deth withdraweth hum fro pruyde
> Ne parteth with þe pore, as puyr charite wolde,
> Bote in gaynesse and in glotonye forglotten here godes
> And breketh nat here bred to þe pore, as þe boke hoteth:
> *Frange esurienti panem tuum.*
>
>   (XI.53-67a)

If this passage seems full of commonplaces, that is probably because what the passage says has required saying in almost every place and time. Nonetheless, in conjunction with all the other evidence we have seen of Langland's reliance on the prophets, we can see how close this passage is to his prophetic forerunners. It begins with a condemnation of empty religiosity, of people from both the courtly and priestly classes who speak of God often but who do not truly believe in godly behavior, at least not for themselves. It condemns those people, much like the false prophets, who delight in discussing complex religious questions to enhance their own glory rather than in teaching true repentance. It condemns those who, in their pride, pray for an end to the plague, God's punishment, but who do not show any sign of reformation, who continue to amass wealth with no concern for the poor. Because of their actions, because of the society's moral and religious deficiencies, even the good will have to suffer. These lines contain no fine theological doctrines that might be interesting subjects for debate. They constitute, rather, a frontal attack on a society that is self-seeking, hypocritical, and unrepentant, a society that to Langland's eyes must have seemed like a fourteenth-century Judah awaiting further punishment and in desperate need of correction.

Langland is not, however, opposed to prayer, just as the prophets are not opposed to ritual. His objections are to empty prayer, to prayer unsupported by true belief and by action. As Liberum Arbitrium explains about charity,

> "A frende he hath þat fynd him þat faylede hym neuere:
> Oen *Aperis-tu-manum* alle thynges hym fyndeth;
> *Fiat-voluntas-tua* festeth hum vch a daye.
> And also a can clergie, *credo-in-deum-patrem*,
> And purtraye well þe *pater-noster* and peynten hit with
>   *auees*.
> And oþer-while his wone is to wynde in pilgrimages
> There pore men and prisones ben, and paye for here fode,

Clotheth hem and conforteth hem and of Crist precheth
hem. . . ."

(XVI.316-23)

Charity lives by prayer, but also by doing. In this passage Langland has brought
together Reason's description of true pilgrimage, visiting the sick and the poor
(IV.122-23), and Will's description of his own activities as one who says many
prayers (V.82-88, where Will cites some of the same prayers mentioned by
Liberum Arbitrium). As we saw in the prophets and in Christ's combination of
"Thou shalt love the lord thy God" and "Thou shalt love thy neighbor as thyself,"
love of God and love of others are inseparable. One without the other is a
mockery; but it is easier to appear to love God by performing rituals, by going
on pilgrimages, than it is to translate that love into an active concern for other
people. The easy religion of empty rituals is hypocritical and forms the major
target of Langland's prophetic attack on his society and its institutions.

3. THE ENDING END OF ALL EARTHLY KNOWING

One of the problems in treating the prophets as social reformers is that their
program seems so vague. If we recognize that a society is failing, we want a
program whereby that society can be reformed; but the prophets are utopians,
and utopians are not always helpful, and are seldom practical, in such areas.
Blenkinsopp says of Ezekiel, "The general impression gained by a reading of
the book as a whole is that moral guidelines are related directly to the kind of
community Israel was intended to be. Hence the starting point is the special
relationship with Israel's God. . . . In keeping with the priestly ethic in the
Pentateuch and the Holiness Code (Lev. 17-26), there is no distinguishing in
principle between ethical and ritual. . . . The ethical teaching of Ezekiel, and of
the prophets in general, presupposes an intrinsic relation between morality and
worship" (200). Blenkinsopp is right, and he points out an important factor in
the prophets' apparent vagueness. They are always positing their preaching on
a pre-existent code. (We may argue, of course, that that code was not the
Pentateuch as we now have it, but the Middle Ages would have thought it was.)
Thus if we ask what constitutes that "intrinsic relationship between morality and
worship," the answer is to be found in the Pentateuch. Similarly, if we ask the
meaning of Isaiah's "Learn to do well," the answer is available through the Bible.
Isaiah's examples are there to remind us of what we are taught elsewhere, to
emphasize the importance of moral action as part of the right relationship with
God. This is the point, too, of Will's search for Dowel, Dobet, and Dobest: we

should already know what they mean; but because we have forgotten, as Langland shows in the first half of the poem, he will use the second half to explore their meaning and to remind us of it. The first half, the "Visio," then, is based on the early chapters of Isaiah, and the second half is a kind of commentary on the first half.

Robert Adams, in his excellent article "Piers's Pardon and Langland's Semi-Pelagianism," discusses the relationship between works and grace and concludes that Langland took a "semi-Pelagian" position by accepting the value of works. While Adams' discussion is very helpful, his emphasis on the theological heresy is perhaps overstated. Because Langland was writing as a poet-prophet, there is no point in trying to fit him into a theological mode. His concern, like that of the prophets, was not with doctrinal orthodoxy. He was concerned with what was right, and he, like the prophets, could not live with the theological distinction between works and grace. They were inseparable. As we shall see, Langland extended his doctrine about the need for action, for doing, to every aspect of life, and his program for reform involved what we might call commitment and engagement. Before we try to understand what Langland meant by Dowel, Dobet, and Dobest, we must recognize how insistent he was on the "Do" aspect of those names.

Several of Langland's allegorical speakers address the question of works, and while the full meaning of "doing well" may remain somewhat vague, there is no equivocation about the need to "do." Dame Study, for instance, tells Will

> "Nowe is þe manere at þe mete, when munstrals ben stile,
> The lewed aȝen þe lered þe holy lore to dispute,
> And tellen of þe trinite how two slowe þe thridde
> And brynge forth ballede resones, taken Bernard to
>   witnesse,
> And putten forth presumpcioun to preue þe sothe.
> Thus they dreuele at the deyes, the deite to knowe,
> And gnawen god with gorge when here gottes fullen.
> Ac þe carfole may crye and quake at þe ȝate,
> Bothe afyngred and afurst, and for defaute spille;
> Is non so hende to haue hym yn, but hote hum go þer god is!
> Thenne semeth hit to my sihte, to suche þat so biddeth,
> God is nat in þat hoem, ne his helpe nother."
> (XI.35-46)

These are indeed people who have god "muche in her mouth ac mene in her herte." Furthermore, all their theological speculation is doubly evil. Not only do they spend their time discussing the nature of God to the exclusion of caring for the poor, but their speculations lead them into clear heresy. If they would busy themselves with deeds rather than with words, both God and His help would be in their homes. Like his prophetic forerunners, Langland is not the least bit subtle on this point. As Ymagenatif says,

> "Ac grace ne groweth nat til gode-will gyue reyne
> And woky thorw gode werkes wikkede hertes . . . .
> So grace withouten grace of god and also gode werkes
> May nat be, be þow syker, thogh we bidde euere."
>
> (XIV.24-25, 28-29)

and Liberum Arbitrium adds

> "The wittiore þat eny wihte is, but yf he worche þeraftur,
> The bittorere he shal abugge, but yf he wel worche."
>
> (XVI.219-20)

After such clear statements, there can be no question about Langland's emphasis on the necessity of doing. Grace without good works is unthinkable. One comes from the divine-human realm and the other comes from the interpersonal realm, and for Langland, as they were for the prophets, those realms are inextricably bound together. It is simply too easy to depend on grace and ignore human responsibilities, and Langland will have none of it. As Langland put it in the B-Text,

> It is lighter to leeue in þre louely persones
> Than for to louye and lene as wel lorels as lele.
>
> (B.XVII.46-47)

In addition, if a person knows what is right and is content with that knowledge without actually using it, that person is betraying human responsibilities. The acquisition of knowledge is not an end in itself. Philip Sidney stated this particular view well when he said that "the highest end of the mistres Knowledge . . . stands (as I thinke) in the knowledge of mans selfe, in the Ethicke and politick consideration, with the end of well dooing and not of well knowing onely . . . so that, the ending end of all earthly learning [is] vertuous action. . . " (161).[4]

Langland, in fact, is quite emphatic about the role of learning in the practice of doing well, and we must remember that the whole experience of *Piers Plowman*, for both Will and the reader, consists of learning. In fact, Langland's concern with learning derives again at least in part from Isaiah, for the important phrase from Isaiah that forms the basis of so much of *Piers Plowman* is not simply "Do well," but "Learn to do well," which Langland understands as "Learn to do well and then do it." The second half of the poem, along with much of the first half, consists precisely of Will's attempts to learn what it means to do well. Will's desire to learn is evident from the very beginning when he asks Holy Church to teach him "How y may saue my soule," and though the question itself is somewhat misguided with its totally egocentric focus, it marks the start of Will's education. Furthermore, Isaiah tells his audience not only that they must learn to do well, but that they must "cease to do perversely." These are two separate commands, and Langland mirrors them when he has Will ask Holy Church to "Kenne me by sum craft to knowe þe false" (II.4). He must know both good and evil.

The problem with learning, as with so many other things in the poem, is that it has become corrupt; and because it has been misused, it has become an object of suspicion. At the poem's end, Langland provides a graphic illustration of the state of learning, when Envy, as a response to Conscience's condemnation

> heete freres go to scole
> And lerne logyk and lawe and eke contemplacioun
> And preche men of Plato and preuen hit by Seneca
> That alle thynges vnder heuene ouhte to be in comune.
> (XXII.273-76)

Not only do the friars neglect their obligation to learn to do well, but they use — or misuse — logic in order to satisfy their envy. Thus Langland is justifiably suspicious of excessive learning, and he recognizes that the solution to the problems he sees in his society does not lie simply in learning. As Conscience tells the friars,

> "ȝow shal no thyng lakke
> With þat ȝe leue logyk and lerneth for to louye."
> (XXII.249-50)

It has been the friars' practice to prove logically, relying on such moralistic sources as Plato and Seneca, that their own pernicious doctrines are correct, but Conscience tells them that they must abandon this course and learn to love. Just as for Augustine belief precedes understanding, so for Langland love must precede learning: "Lerneth to louye" is not different from learn to do well, and if one learns to love, or undertakes learning out of love, learning to do well will necessarily follow. Langland will have no part of scholastic subtleties that serve only to obscure the truth and lead one away from the natural, inherent ability to learn to do well:

> Hit is a kynde knowynge that kenet in thyn herte
> For to louye thy lord leuest of alle,
> Dey rather þen do eny dedly synne.
> (I.141-43)

When Isaiah says, "Learn to do well," he is talking about "kynde knowynge," a natural knowledge that has been perverted by, among other forces, the religious and political leaders. Langland extends this condemnation specifically to the friars, who were known for their learning and for their ability to misuse logic.

Furthermore, Langland is scornful of any learning that does not lead to doing well, including all kinds of metaphysical speculation. Thus when Reason shows Will "þe myrour of Mydelerthe" (XIII.131), Will raises a metaphysical question: why do human beings not follow the dictates of reason? Will seems ready to sit down and have a long chat about the nature of reason and the nature of human beings, but Reason responds by quoting Ecclesiasticus 11:9, "Strive not in a matter which doth not concern thee . . ." and Ymagenatif explains that

> "Adam, þe whiles he spak nat, hadde paradys at wille,
> Ac when he mamelede aboute mete and musede for to
>   knowe
> The wisdom and the wit of god, he was pot out of blisse.
> Rihte so ferde Resoun by the for thy rude speche,
> And for thow woldest wyte why of Resones preuete."
>
>   (XIII.224-48)

Such inquiries into the "wisdom and the wit of god" or the nature of reason have nothing to do with learning to do well, with fulfilling our human responsibilities, and they are therefore not worth asking. This apparently anti-intellectual attitude, of course, must be understood in the context of Langland's condemnation of all who, like the friars, use their learning and their metaphysical speculations to distort the meaning of scripture, manipulating it for their own purposes, overcoming the scruples of conscience, and putting both individuals and nation into peril. Again, the purpose behind learning is doing, which people seem to have forgotten.

The attack on learning made by Recklessness, therefore, is not so much an attack on learning itself as on its distortions. Like so much that Recklessness says, it is an overreaction, but it is not without foundation. Recklessness is correct, for instance, in saying that if people had to live according to everything that Scripture and Clergy teach, no one would make it to heaven. To deny this would be to deny the efficacy of grace. It does not follow, however, that learning is unimportant, if it is learning to do well. Even Recklessness admits that "ho-so doth by 3oure doctrine doth wel" (XI.226), but rather than doing well he would prefer to rely on grace. He has been discouraged by seeing supposedly learned men "more sette here herte/In goed than in god" (XI.231-32) and he accurately points out that

> "Wel ywitted men and wel ylettred clerkes,
> Seldom ar they seyen so lyue as they lere."
>
> (XI.236-37)

To rule out the value of learning because it is difficult to do what one learns or because so many people do not do it is indeed a reckless view, one that is soon corrected by Ymagenatif, who, as Pearsall notes, reconciles "faith and grace with reason and good works" (234-35) by recognizing the important role of learning in doing well. After all, as Ymagenatif points out, "Al-pei3 men make bokis god was here mayster" (XIV.46) and a "kynde-witted man" cannot arrive at the truths of Christianity unless he is taught by clerks. Thus

> grace is a gifte of god and kynde wit a chaunce
> And clergie a connynge of kynde wittes techyng.
>
> (XIV.33-34)

All three, grace, kynde wit, and clergy, are necessary; they are not, as Reckless-ness implied, opposing forces. Consequently

> Well may þe barne blesse þat hym to boek sette,
> That lyuynge aftur lettrure saued hym lyf and soule!
>
> (XIV.126-27)

The point here is not just that learning is a good thing. It is that the person who learns and who then lives accordingly, the person who learns to do well and then does it, gains salvation. As always, Langland refuses to accept easy solutions. We cannot rely only on grace or only on learning. The two work together, and require translation into action. A further implication of this position is that study must be undertaken in a particularly intense way, a way that indicates that it will be translated into proper action. This is the import of Study's initial attack on Will:

> "Wel artow wyse," quod she to Wyt, "suche wysdomes to
>   shewe
> To eny foel or to flaterere or to frentike peple!"
> And sayde: *"Nolite mittere*, 3e men, margerie-perles
> Among hogges þat han hawes at wille;
> They do bote dreuele theron — draf were hem leuere
> Then al þe preciouse perye þat eny prince weldeth.
> Y syg hit by suche," quod she, "þat sheweth by here werkes

> Thei louyen lond and lordschipe and lykynge of body
> More then holynesse or hendenesse or al þat seyntes
>   techeth."
>
> (XI.5-13)

Study takes the advice about throwing pearls before swine seriously, because the swine that "dreuele theron" are like the lewd scholars who engage in theological speculations and "dreuele at the deyes." Study's anger results from her observations of the "werkes" of such scholars, which works are clearly evil. The implication is that they use their learning to justify their attraction to land, lordship, and bodily pleasure. It is only when Will promises her that he will translate her teachings into appropriate actions — "to worche 3oure wille þe while my lyf dureth" (XI.91) — that she gives him the directions to Clergy, which require him to avoid Rychesse, women, wine, wrath, ire, and sloth so that he can arrive at "Soffre-Bothe-wele-and-wo-yf-þou-wilt-lerne" (XI.107-8). These directions, so much like Piers's directions to Truth, underscore another of Study's reasons for being upset with Wit. Wit's instructions were too easy, too freely given. They allowed Will simply to ask and be told. He was not required to put forth any effort. People who are content with such learning — and Study thinks that Will is one of them — tend to be content with superficial learning. True learning requires doing. This, too, is the point of Conscience's words to Clergy:

> "By Crist," quod Consience, "Clergie, y wol nat lye,
> Me were leuere, by oure lorde, and y leue sholde,
> Haue pacience parfitlyche than half thy pak of bokes!"
>
> (XV.178-80)

Conscience does not condemn learning — after all, he still wants to keep half of Clergy's books. What he condemns is that kind of learning that confines itself only to learning and ignores doing. Conscience's desire to supplement the books with "pacience," from the Latin *patior*, to suffer, refers directly back to Study's "Soffre-bothe-wel-and-wo . . . " and illustrates the consistency of Langland's thought on this matter. Learning without doing well is not true learning.

The other side of this issue, of course, involves teaching; and because teachers were members of the Church, it involves the priesthood as well:

> Riht so oute of holy churche al evel spredeth
> There inparfit preesthoed is, prechares and techares.
>
> (XVI.245-46)

Both the friars of Passus X and the doctor of Passus XV have an intellectual knowledge of Dowel, but none of them act on it. As Liberum Arbitrium says, "to prechen and preue hit nat — ypocrisye hit semeth" (XVI.263), and such hypocrisy is especially harmful in people who are supposed to set examples, for, as Patience tells the doctor, the nation regards teachers such as himself as leaders "and liue as thow techest" (XV.170). His teaching consists of both what he expounds *and* what he does; and if there is a distinction between those two, the nation will learn that lesson. Consequently, to teach well also requires that one do well:

> And suche liue as þei lereth men, our lord Treuthe hem
> graunteth
> To be peres to þe apostles . . .
> (IX.19-20)

It should be clear by now that Langland applies the criterion of doing to every aspect of life covered in *Piers Plowman*. As the prophets consistently point out, it would be easy to fulfill God's teachings if those teachings required no more than talk, but they require action as well. This is Langland's point, too:

> "How?" quod alle þe comune, "thow conseylest vs to ʒelde
> Al þat we owen eny wyhte or þat we go to hosele?"
> "That is my conseil," quod Consience, "and cardinale
> vertues;
> Or vch man forʒeue oþer, and þat wol þe *pater-noster*,
> *Et dimitte nobis debita nostra . . .* "
> (XXI.391-94a)

The "comune" are astounded that they are being told not only to say the Pater Noster but to do what it says. That such a command seems so revolutionary to them is sufficient commentary on the state of the nation.

Langland's emphasis on the need for doing runs from one end of the poem to the other, and it forms part of every important scene. Near the beginning we read

> For Iames þe gentele iugeth in his bokes
> That fayth withouten þe feet is feblore then nautht
> And as ded as dore-nayl but yf þe dedes folowe . . .
> For this aren wordes ywryten in þe ewangelie:
> "*Date et dabitur vobis* — for y dele ʒow alle."
> And þat is þe lok of loue and vnloseth grace . . .
> (I.181-83, 196-98)

and at the end, "Ac wel worth Peres the plouhman þat pursueth god in doynges" (XXI.430). And surely one of the major ways of doing well, following the prophets, involves caring for the poor and helpless: "Forthy y rede ȝow riche, haueth reuthe uppon þe poor" (I.171), as Holy Church says. Thus in order to avail themselves of the Pardon, the merchants are advised to

> bugge boldly what hem best likede
> And sethe sullen hit aȝeyn and saue þe wynnynges,
> Amende meson-dewes þerwith . . .
> And brugges tobrokene by the heye wayes
> Amende in som manere wyse and maydones helpe,
> Pore peple bedredene and prisones in stokkes
> Fynde hem for goddes loue. . . .
>
>   (IX.28-35)

This advice corresponds to Jesus' words to the young man who is seeking salvation, "Sell what thou hast, and give to the poor, and thou shalt have treasures in heaven" (Matthew 19:21). Like the young man, the merchants can attain salvation by performing charitable acts in both the religious and secular spheres. The reciprocity involved here may seem heretical in limiting God's ability to confer grace; but again, Langland is not terribly concerned about the theological niceties of his position. *Piers Plowman* is not a long refutation of Bradwardine; it is an attempt to reform society, for the "comune profit," so that all can be saved. And clearly it is part of the "comune profit" to care for the poor, not simply because it can lead to salvation but because justice itself is desirable. As Piers tells the women, part of their task is to make cloth "For profit of the pore and plesaunce of ȝowsuluen" (VIII.14). His point is not so much that women enjoy making cloth as that helping the poor provides "plesaunce." All of his recommendations, he tells them, are "for ȝoure profit."

Langland recognizes that the problem is not quite so simple when he discusses, in Passus VIII and IX, the differences between the truly deserving and false beggars. While recognizing that there are cheats among the beggars, Langland seems to leave the determination of who they are up to God, for "þai haue no part of pardoun, ne of preyere ne of penaunces" (IX.174), whereas for the deserving poor

> For loue of here lowe hertes oure lord hath hem ygraunted
> Here penaunce and here purgatorye vppon this puyre erthe
> And pardon with the plouhman *a pena et a culpa.*
>
>   (IX.184-86)

Those fakers who are obvious about it can be denied sustenance (VIII.124-27), but if there is any doubt about whether a beggar is a fraud, that person should be helped. It is up to God, finally, to determine who are the deserving poor.

Langland's attitude toward deeds is also apparent in the brief Trajan episode. Ruth Morse says, "Langland seems to want to say . . . that while salvation and grace are a mystery, it is still possible to merit God's free gift by good works" (28). Actually Langland's position seems to be a bit more extreme: because salvation and grace are a mystery, we must devote our attention to something that we more clearly understand, good works. Because of his good works, Trajan could be saved, even without "syngynge of mo masses" or "lele bileue" (XII.84-85). However complicated the Trajan story may have become in other versions, Langland's use of it is fairly straightforward, and it illustrates the points to which he frequently returns throughout *Piers Plowman*: people must, for the good of society and for their own salvation, learn to do well. Langland, as we saw, is not saying anything new here, though he is saying it effectively. For example, in the country called *Cor-hominis* grows a tree called Trewe-love,

> And þerof cometh a goed fruyt, þe whiche men calleth
> werkes
> Of holynesse, of hendenesse, of helpe-hym-þat-nedeth,
> The whiche is *Caritas* ykald, Cristes oune fode. . . .
> (XVIII.12-14)

Not only does the tree grow in the human heart, but Will's guide is Liberum Arbitrium, free will. It is up to each human being, functioning as both an individual and as a member of society, to choose to perform charitable works. Only thus can society continue to operate and thus can the individual seek salvation. Langland could have discovered these ideas in many places, but the unique combination of form and message, tone and technique, could only have come from his direct knowledge of the prophets and from his feeling that he, too, must deliver the prophetic message to a deeply troubled society.

4. DOWEL, DOBET, DOBEST

One of the vexing problems in *Piers Plowman* criticism involves the understanding of Dowel, Dobet, and Dobest. Before we actually take another look at those concepts, there are a number of points we should consider.

Several attempts have been made at understanding these concepts based on external factors like the Active, Contemplative, and Mixed lives (Wells) or the

Father, Son, and Holy Ghost (Frank); but in light of Langland's reliance on and development of the prophets, such external schemes are not necessary. Nor is it necessary to view the poem's second half as a quest. Not only would it be a quest with "many beginnings, no middle, and an ambiguous end" (Muscatine 78-79), but it "turns out to be not a search for something but an opportunity to expose the shortcomings of society when measured against the standards of Truth" (Fowler 255-56). It is, furthermore, an opportunity for Langland to try to explain and extend that central concept from Isaiah, Learn to do well. We must also remember that "Dowel" is a verb not a noun and that Langland's emphasis is on "Do" rather than on "wel," "bet," and "best." It is also important not to create a contest among the three concepts, with Dowel somehow coming out the loser. Dobest is certainly at a higher level than Dowel; but the prophet's instruction is to learn to do well, and if a society could just follow that instruction, how much better it would be! Still, no matter how good we think we are (and Will at least hints that he considered himself "a parfit man"), we can never become complacent, because Dobet and Dobest are always beckoning. And after all, Dowel, Dobet, and Dobest differ not in kind but in degree. They are all variations of the same qualities.

Finally, we must realize that the definitions and examples of the three kinds of doing that Will receives are not mutually exclusive. When Isaiah says "Learn to do well," he provides, as we saw, examples of doing well: seeking justice, relieving the oppressed, helping the powerless. From these examples we can begin to understand what he means by doing well. So, too, with Langland: from the various definitions and examples, we can begin to understand what he means by Dowel, Dobet, and Dobest. It is impossible, however, to provide one inclusive definition for each term because such moral concepts are inevitably vague. When they become too clearly defined, when they are transformed into a set of rules, they become not only oversimplified but also subject to legalistic interpretation. By keeping the terms slightly vague, by showing them from different perspectives, Langland challenges his audience to redefine them, to interpret them in a variety of situations, to make them not just a series of rules to follow (or about which to rationalize) but an organic part of their everyday lives. He is not providing a scholastic discussion of the virtues and vices. He is providing a prescription for the salvation of individuals and societies, and that prescription requires that we not only learn but that we do, like the "comune" in Passus XXI who are shocked to learn that they must do what the *Pater noster* says.

One of the clearest places to begin examining the meaning of these confusing terms is in the definitions provided by the doctor, who knows what the words mean even if he does not put his knowledge into practice:

> "Y have yseide," quod þat segg, "y can sey no bettre,
> Bote do as doctours techeth for Dowel y hit holde;

> That trauayleth to teche oþere y halde hit for a Dobet;
> And he þat doth as he techeth, y halde hit for þe beste."
>
> (XV.124-27)

To do as the doctors teach is to do well, to teach others is to do better, and to do as one teaches is to do best. If we understand the differences among these activities, we can understand Langland's terms.

To do as the doctors teach is to follow the teachings of the Church. This practice is obviously a good one. It requires learning what the doctors teach and caring about it enough to follow it. This step is vital for individual salvation but it is also largely limited to individual salvation. The person who takes this step does well; and if everyone did it, society would be nearer perfection. But everyone does not know that step or what it requires. Consequently, it would be better if those who do know it would teach it. This second step, because it is directed toward others, goes beyond the first step in degree. And it would be even better — that is to say, best — if the person who taught others also abided by his or her own teaching. Not only would such a person be teaching by example as well as by words, but that person's actions would be inclusive, incorporating both self and others, individual and societal salvation.

The doctor himself, of course, provides a negative example of his own definitions, for while he teaches accurately in words, his actions violate what he teaches. Intellectually he knows what he is saying, but he does not internalize his own teaching. It is not really a part of him. This hypocrisy angers Clergy, but the sudden appearance of Piers supports what the doctor has said, for Piers largely reiterates the doctor's words:

> "Byfore perpetuel pees y shal preue þat y saide
> And avowe byfore god, and forsaken hit neuere,
> That *disce, doce, dilige deum*
> And thyn enemy helpe emforth thy myhte."
>
> (XV.139-42)

Although Piers never mentions the "do" triad, he is clearly referring to the doctor's definitions, and his own explanations differ little from the doctor's: learn, teach, and serve God. Again learning is individual, teaching is other-directed, and serving God is inclusive. Piers's example of serving God is to help one's enemy, both by correcting that person with words (that is, by teaching) and by providing material aid (that is, by example and by doing). Piers simply offers a concrete illustration of what the doctor calls doing as one teaches. It can lead to both individual salvation and the betterment of society, which then makes individual salvation more easily attainable. These levels of behavior, like the relationship between the individual and society, are intertwined. Dowel, Dobet, and Dobest go together; what is truly best for the individual is also best

for the "comune profit," and what is best for the "comune profit" is best for the
individual.

We can see this same pattern repeated in all of the other attempts to explain
the "do" triad. Thus Wit explains to Will, "Ho-so lyueth in lawe and in loue doth
wel" (X.202). That individual who lives in law and love does well, which is
certainly the case, but such a life is only a beginning:

> "And thenne dede we alle wel, and wel bet ȝut to louye
> Oure enemyes enterely and helpe hem at here nede.
> And ȝut were best to ben aboute and brynge hit to hepe
> That alle landes loueden and in on lawe bileuede."
>
> (X.187-90)

If we all lived in love and law, that would be good for us as individuals; but if we
loved our enemies and helped them, that, as an activity directed toward others,
would be even better; and best of all would be if we would help everyone else
to believe in law and love.

It is immediately obvious that Piers includes helping one's enemies as part
of Dobest, whereas Wit cites it as part of Dobet. This apparent inconsistency
does not mean, however, that the characters contradict each other or that
Langland was confused. Rather, it is important to see that the specific points
are not as important as the patterns that they form. Like Isaiah's examples of
doing well, these are only examples; and this set of examples follows the same
pattern as the previous ones. Living in love and law is fine for us as individuals,
but helping our enemies benefits others; and getting everyone to believe in law
and love, through our words and our actions, benefits all of us. Wit makes this
pattern even clearer at the end of the passus:

> "And thus is Dowel, my frende, to do as lawe techeth,
> To louye and to loue the and no lyf to greue.
> Ac to louye and to lene, leef me, þat is Dobet.
> Ac to ȝeue and to ȝeme bothe ȝonge and olde,
> Helen and helpen, is Dobest of alle.
> For þe more a man may do, by so þat a do hit,
> The more he is worthy and worth, of wyse and of goed
>   ypresed."
>
> (X.301-07)

Dowel is to follow the law and love, to harm no one else. It focuses on the
individual. Dobet is to extend that love so that it becomes an active force, not
so that it does no harm but so that it actually does good for others, in the form
of lending aid. Dobest is to extend that love even further, to make it a more
active force, so that rather than lending aid, we give it freely. Again, the pattern

is individual, other, all of us; and Wit's conclusion, that the more a man may do, as long as he actually does it, the worthier he is, illustrates Langland's constant emphasis on doing. All of the kinds of doing that Wit enumerates are good. They differ only in the degree of active doing. This is the case with all of the definitions that the various characters provide throughout the second half of *Piers Plowman*, as a brief survey will show.

The first set of definitions comes from Thought, according to whom Dowel follows the person

> "Ho is trewe of his tonge and of his two handes
> And thorw lele labour lyueth and loueth his emcristene
> And therto trewe of his tyl and takeþ but his owene
> And is nat dronklewe ne dedeynous. . . ."
>
> (X.78-81)

This definition recalls Holy Church's answer to Will's question of how to save his soul:

> "For who is trewe of his tonge and of his two handes
> And doth þe werkes þerwith and wilneth no man ylle,
> He is a god by þe gospel. . . ."
>
> (I.84-86)

Doing well is indeed the way to save one's soul and is obviously vital; but if one does all this and in addition actively helps other people by overcoming Avarice and by preaching and teaching, one goes beyond doing well and does better. And if one goes even further than caring for other individuals and becomes, like a true bishop, concerned for the whole of society, one does best. Again we see the same pattern of care for individual, other, and society that characterizes all the definition of the "Do" triad.

Ymagenatif, too, though he only specifically defines Dowel and Dobet, employs the pattern. For Ymagenatif, that person does well who does not beguile others, who does not lie, teach what is forbidden, talk too much, or waste time, but who is humble and follows the law. That person does better who loves, lends, lives well, who does all the things we call charity, who promotes peace, patience, and Christian poverty. Once more, Dowel focuses on the individual's actions as they apply to the self while Dobet focuses on the individual's actions as they apply to others. And though Ymagenatif does not define Dobest, he does refer to

> vnkynde rychesse —
> As loreles to be lordes and lewede men techares

> And holy chirche horen helpe, auerous and coueytous —
> Druyeth vp Dowel and distruyeth Dobest.
>
> (XIV.19-22)

Dowel will dry up and Dobest will be destroyed by such societal failures as unworthy lords and teachers and the failure of the Church, all of which result from "vnkynde richesse." Not only does Ymagenatif here repeat the pattern, but he also illustrates the kind of connections that exist among the three "Do's," to which we will return soon.

First, however, we can see that Patience's definitions also fit into the pattern:

> And these ben Dowel and Dobet and Dobest of alle.
> *Cordis contricio* cometh of sorughe of herte
> And *oris confessio*, þat cometh of shrifte of mouthe
> And satisfaccion, þat for soules paieth and for alle synnes
> quyteth.
>
> (XVI.28-31)

Dowel requires individuals to search their hearts and recognize their sins; Dobet requires them to confess those sins to others; and Dobest requires some specific act of satisfaction. Here again we can see the pattern of increased doing, moving from the individual to others.

One of the most striking examples of the pattern comes in Passus XXI.108-98, when Conscience describes the "Do" triad in terms of Christ's life: when Christ turned the water to wine ("For wyn is likned to lawe and lyf-holinesse") he did well; when he wrought miracles, curing the lame and the blind and feeding the multitude, he did better; and when he established the Church, he did best. Each step here represents a movement outward from the individual and the observance of law to the salvation of society. Furthermore, each step corresponds to the appropriate division in the "Vita" section of the poem. The vision of Dowel largely concerns Will's attempts to understand what Dowel means by examining himself, his own internal faculties, by looking in his heart. The vision of Dobet, telling of Faith, Hope, and Charity, and culminating with the Crucifixion, shows concern for others, but still stresses individual sacrifice and salvation. And the vision of Dobest, describing the history and problems of the Church, moves to the societal realm. Again we see the development from self to other to society, as well as an interpretation of the Crucifixion: Christ died to make salvation possible, but his sacrifice requires active cooperation both on individual and societal levels to make salvation a reality; both as individuals and as a society, we must learn to do well, better, and best.

After this attempt to delineate what Langland meant by Dowel, Dobet, and Dobest, we must also consider the limits of the delineation. We must remember that the elements in this triad differ not in kind but in degree. They are all variations on the same theme. Consequently, even if these elements do not correspond to the persons of the Trinity, as Frank argues, they are like the persons of the Trinity in being inseparable. If a person does well, truly does well, by loving and living according to the law, such a person automatically will do better and do best, for the law requires that we care for each other on individual and communal levels. This lesson, as we saw, was one of the major teachings of the prophets. Thus Clergy tells Will

> "By Crist," quod Clergie, "yf thow coueyte Dowel
> Kepe þe ten comaundementis and kepe þe fro synne
> And byleef lely how goddes sone alyhte
> On þe maide Marie for mankynde sake
> And bycam a man of þat maide withoute mankynde.
> And al þat holi churche herof can þe lere
> Leue hit lely and loke þou do þeraftur."
>
> (XI.142-48)

Keep the Ten Commandments and believe in Christ's Incarnation; and everything that Holy Church can teach about all this, *believe* it and *do* it. If individuals follow Clergy's advice about achieving Dowel, then Dobet and Dobest must necessarily follow, for selves, others, and societies, like Dowel, Dobet, and Dobest, are inextricably tied together. As Ymagenatif pointed out, if there is no Dowel, there can be no Dobest. And since all salvation is linked, both individual and societal, we must now consider the basis of Dowel, individual responsibility.

5. THE ROLE OF THE INDIVIDUAL

The role of the individual and the relationship between the individual and society are treated frequently in the Bible; but because these matters are complex, the biblical treatment of them is also complex. For instance, in Exodus 20:5-6 we read, "I am the Lord thy God . . . visiting the iniquity of the fathers upon the children, unto the third and fourth generation of them that hate me: And shewing mercy unto thousands to them that love me, and keep my commandments." These verses seem to say that children will either suffer or be rewarded according to the actions of their parents. On the other hand, Deuteronomy 24:16 says, "The fathers shall not be put to death for the children, nor the children for the fathers, but every one shall die for his own sin." The apparent contradiction between these two passages reveals a recognition of the complex relationship between individual responsibility and the role of society. All individuals are responsible for their own behavior, as Deuteronomy teaches, and yet individual behavior is obviously determined in large part by one's environment, as Exodus implies. The implications of these passages are specifically addressed in Ezekiel 18, in which the prophet examines the proverb "The fathers have eaten sour grapes and the teeth of the children are set on edge." Ezekiel's point is that the proverb is mistaken, that despite environmental influences, each individual is responsible for his or her own behavior. He begins by describing a just man in terms that should remind us of Langland's descriptions of Dowel, Dobet, and Dobest:

> 5. And if a man be just, and do judgment and justice. . . . 7.
> And hath not wronged any man: but hath restored the
> pledge to the debtor, hath taken nothing away by violence:
> hath given his bread to the hungry, and hath covered the
> naked with a garment: 8. Hath not lent upon usury, nor
> taken any increase: hath withdrawn his hand from iniquity,
> and hath executed true judgment between man and man: 9.
> Hath walked in my commandments, and kept my judg-
> ments, to do truth: he is just, he shall surely live, saith the
> Lord God.

But if such a paragon has a son who does not live so well, who grieves "the needy and the poor," that son "shall surely die, his blood shall be upon him" (13). Similarly, if a wicked father has a good son, the son will not be punished for his father's sins.

While Ezekiel's point is clear and reassuring, its applicability is not always obvious to us as we view the world. Ezekiel himself shortly before had condemned Jerusalem by saying, "As the mother was, so also is the daughter" (16:44), and Jeremiah (to choose one of many possible examples) wonders "Why doth the way of the wicked prosper: why is it well with all them that transgress, and wickedly?" (12:1). If each person is responsible for his or her own sins, why do the wicked prosper? This is the kind of metaphysical question that we cannot answer, and it is important to note that Jeremiah prefaces the question by declaring "Thou indeed, O Lord, art just, if I plead with thee." Jeremiah begins by affirming his trust in God, which means that he affirms the necessity of behaving properly, according to divine teaching, even if he cannot always see the consequences that he expects.

If the emphasis in such passages is on individual responsibility, how, then, are we to understand the relationship between the individual and society? It is clear, for instance, in Isaiah that the nation is being threatened and will be punished because they "consume my people and grind the faces of the poor" (3:15). Not only are these both individual and societal failures, but when the punishment comes — whether it be in the form of a plague or a conquest by a foreign power — the poor and the righteous will suffer as well as the wicked. The Babylonians and Assyrians did not exempt the poor and the righteous. The whole nation suffered the consequences of wickedness. Thus, while individual responsibility is basic, the prophets also convey a sense of collective responsibility and suffering. Individuals are responsible for their own behavior and for their society, while the society is also responsible for the behavior of individuals. They are inseparable, though their foundation lies with the individual.

This is a point that Langland makes frequently. For example, three times he says, possibly paraphrasing Tobias 3:6, "Melius est mori quam male vivere," it is better to die than to live badly (I.143a; VI.290a; XVII.40a). The third time, Liberum Arbitrium explains what this entails:

> "This is no more to mene bote men of holy churche
> Sholde reseue riht nauht but þat riht wolde
> And refuse reuerences and raueners offrynges.
> Thenne wolde lordes and ladyes be loth for to agulte
> And to take of here tenauntes more then treuthe wolde,
> And marchauntz merciable wolde be and men of lawe
>   bothe,
> Wolde religious refuse rauenours almesses.
> And thenne grace sholde growe ȝut and grene-leued wexe
> And charite þat chield is now sholde chaufen of humsulue
> And conforte alle cristene, wolde holy churche amende."
>   (XVII.41-50)

If churchmen, as teachers and exemplars, would reform by accepting responsibility for their actions, then individuals in the other estates would do the same and the society as a whole would function properly, and it is significant that the C-Text focuses increased attention on the responsibilities of churchmen, beginning with the addition of the story of Ophni and Phinees (Prol.106-07). The choice is between living badly or doing well, and it is no accident that this particular explanation is provided by Liberum Arbitrium, free will, for each individual must, through the power of free will, choose which way to live. Holy Church may use the proverbial "Talis pater, talis filia" to describe Meed (II.27a), the allegorical daughter of Favel, but the proverb should not be applied to people, who have the ability to choose their way of living. This is why, according to Piers,

> "And yf Grace graunte the to go in in thys wyse
> Thow shalt se Treuthe sitte in thy sulue herte. . . ."
>   (VII.254-55)

The way to Dowel, and therefore to Dobet and Dobest, begins by going into the heart and then moving out, just as Will comes to understand these concepts first by looking within and then considering the world outside himself. And as we saw earlier, in Passus V Will himself must be moved to action, to being more than a spectator. At the beginning of the poem he describes himself as "vnholy of werkes" (Prol.3), which does not mean that he is actively evil but that he has not performed good works. Like so many characters in the poem, Will must learn not just to do well, but to do at all.

Furthermore, the reformation of self is inextricably tied to the reformation of society. The question is not so much which is primary, for they are nearly inseparable. The question is how to accomplish them both, and the answer depends largely on religious reform in the sense of a return to doing what the religion teaches, for the religious teachings pervade the other realms. What Israel Mattuck says about the prophets is equally true for Langland: they were not primarily social reformers, for they did not view social reform as an end in itself; rather, social reform was an integral part of religious reform (96).

This view, to digress briefly, helps to explain the role of Piers himself. Piers's role undergoes some development in the course of the poem; but more than anything else, Piers represents an ideal of the papacy. Because religion holds a central position in its intertwined relationship with politics and morality, and because Langland is therefore a religious reformer, he had to be critical of the papacy, especially with the effects of the Avignon captivity helping to create chaos in the Church. Early in the poem he associates Rome with Simony and Meed, and towards the end he has the "lewed vicory" wishing that

> "no cardinal come among þe comune peple,
> Bote in here holinesse holden hem stille
> At Avenon among Iewes (*cum sancto sanctus eris, etc.*)
> Or in Rome, as here reule wolde, þe relikes to kepe. . . ."
>   (XXI.420-23)

This is not to say that Langland opposed the institution of the papacy, as other reformers did. Rather Langland sought a reformed papacy, including a restoration of humility to that office. Therefore Peter becomes Piers, who is a plowman, with all that that implies about preaching and spreading the word of God. In fact, as Barney notes, "The first word Piers speaks ['Peter' (VII.182)] immediately suggests a link with apostolic tradition, if not the papacy" (287). Thus Piers plays a central role in the establishment of Unity, the Church, and is given control of the Pardon. Grace calls him "my procuratour and my reue . . . My prowour and my plouhman Peres shal ben erthe . . ." (XXI.258-60). In Passus VII it is Piers who knows the way to Truth and early in Passus XXI, after we have seen the early history of the Church and been brought up to the present, it is

Piers who becomes the earthly representative of Christ (and most certainly not Christ himself).

We can see Piers's role defined most clearly in the speech of the "lewed vicory":

> "Inparfit is þat pope þat all peple sholde helpe
> And soudeth hem þat sleeth suche as he sholde saue.
> Ac wel worth Peres the plouhman þat pursueth god in
> doynges . . . .
> Rihte so Peres the plouhman payneth hym to tulie
> As wel for a wastour or for a wenche of the stuyves
> As for hymsulue and his seruauntes. . . .
> And god amende þe pope þat pileth holi churche
> And claymeth bifore þe kynge to be kepare ouer cristene
> And counteth nat thow cristene be culde and yrobbed . . . ."
>
> (XXI.428-44)

The pope who is in office promotes murder, countenances theft, and himself pillages the Church. Piers, on the other hand, the ideal of what the Pope should be, "pursueth god in doynges," surely a significant phrase in light of our approach to the poem: he works as much for others, no matter how socially insignificant they may be, as for himself — in other words, he does well, does better, and, in thereby bringing everyone to salvation, he does best. Piers, in short, lives up to the ideal that Liberum Arbitrium described earlier:

> "For were presthode more parfyte, that is, þe pope formost
> That with moneye maynteyneth men to werre vppon
> cristene
> Aȝen þe lore of our lord as seynt Luk witnesseth,
> *Michi vindictam*,
> His preyeres with his pacience to pees sholde brynge
> Alle londes into loue and þat in lytel tyme;
> The pope with alle prestes *pax vobis* sholde make."
>
> (XVII.233-38)

If the popes and, as a result, the priests should reform, Unity could be reestablished. That they do not is, as the concluding passus show, the failing of the individuals involved. This is why the poem ends with Conscience going off in search of Piers: he is seeking the ideal pope who will restore Unity, the Church, and thereby restore unity in the world. Once again, reform is both individual and societal.

Finally, the responsibility of the individual and the links among the individual, the society, and God, can be seen in the recurrent phrase "*redde quod debes*," which Bloomfield, relying on Aquinas, associates with justice (1961, 131). Since, however, as Bloomfield notes, "*Redde quod debes* . . . is the essence of Truth's pardon" (130), we might do well to see this doctrine of restitution as part of the covenant that God has offered to human beings, for we see its terms repeated throughout the poem. *Redde quod debes* refers, of course, to the human obligation to make proper restitution, to establish justice, to create a perfect society. On the other hand, Holy Church tells Will about charity:

> "For this aren wordes ywryten in þe ewangelie:
> '*Date et dabitur vobis* — for y dele ȝow alle.'
> And þat is þe lok of loue and vnloseth grace. . . ."
>
> (I.195-97)

There is a mutuality in the idea of giving and receiving: we can see it in the pardon, in *redde quod debes*, in *date et dabitur vobis,* in the plowing scene when Piers was "apayed and payede wel hem here huyre" (VIII.115) and we can see it qualified in the warning "Non reddas malum pro malo" (V.58a), which requires us to exercise individual responsibility in not carrying out mutuality if it requires us to do evil. Again, as individuals and as a society, we are obligated by the terms of this covenant. The result for Langland of his understanding of the covenant was not the reform that he wished for, but it was the creation of *Piers Plowman,* a work that, like the works of the prophets, warns, chastises, and berates the society for which it was created.

6. CONCLUSION

Morton Bloomfield closes his invaluable study of *Piers Plowman* by saying, "If I have been able to direct the investigation of *Piers* towards the right questions, even if I have not provided all the answers, I feel that this work has not been in vain" (154). I hope that the present study is a further move in the right direction, that it reveals some new aspects of the poem and that it casts new light on some old questions. In attempting to do so, my approach differs from Bloomfield's in several important ways, though I agree on the vital point of Langland's concern with the welfare of society rather than with a focus on individual salvation. However, as Bloomfield notes, "With Langland, the reader moves in an area of few facts and many contradiction. . . . There are no external facts to provide clues. One is forced back to the text again and to his own sense of literary fitness" (76-77). Apparently my "sense of literary fitness" differs from Bloomfield's, for while he finds the source of *Piers Plowman* in medieval considerations of Christian perfection, influenced by Christian apocalypticism, I see the poem's source in a fairly literal application of the ethical (and hence religious) teachings of the prophets, largely devoid of apocalypticism. Bloomfield says that "the very subject of the poem, Christian perfection, in its social form, bespeaks apocalypticism. Social thinking on the subject of perfection, above all in the fourteenth century, had to be apocalyptic. The transcendence of society to a new level was thought by many to be the only way out of the crushing dilemma" (104). Undoubtedly there were many who felt this way, but Langland was not among them. His focus is not on preparing the way for a new world, and he is not thinking eschatologically. Rather, he is proposing a way in which human beings, working, of course, through God by adhering to divine law, can reform the world. This is what makes him both a revolutionary and a reactionary: he wants to overturn the existing order, not to establish a new order so much as to reestablish an old one, the order that we see, for instance, in the early history of Unity, before present corruption has attacked it. Furthermore, Langland is prophetic in warning the people that they had better reform or they will pay for their sinfulness, as indeed they had already started paying in the form of pestilence and strife.

It is helpful here to refer to Emmerson's distinction between prophetic and apocalyptic texts. Among the differences that Emmerson explores is one between the prophet and the apocalyptic visionary. Whereas the apocalyptic visionary is usually not a participant in the actions he describes but a mere transcriber of visions, the prophet "is a participant in the divine will for Israel, an actor. And sometimes, as in Jeremiah 19:1-5 and Isaiah 20:2-4, he is told to act out what he knows in a kind of street theater" (44). Will, both waking and asleep, is clearly more than a messenger. In a variety of ways, and especially in the second half of the poem, he is an active participant, interacting with characters, journeying, dressing in significant apparel, reflecting on the actions and the conversations that he records. As a participant in his poem, Will is far closer to Isaiah and Jeremiah than he is to the apocalyptic narrators of Revelation or Enoch.

Furthermore, Emmerson notes, "Unlike the prophet who speaks usually to the present, to contemporary circumstances, the visionary despairs of the possibility of change during present oppression and puts his hope in the future" (46). As I have tried to show throughout this study, Langland was speaking precisely to contemporary circumstances in order to bring about individual and societal reform. If he is at all hopeful about the future — and I think he is — it is not because he anticipates imminent divine or eschatological intervention. It is because he thinks that, in human terms, reform is possible. That is why Conscience sets out to find Piers, not an eschatological savior but an ideal religious leader who, like Peter, the original Piers, will be able to restore the Church, teach the terms of the Pardon, be Christ's true earthly representative, and enable brothers to dwell together in Unity.

It is interesting to note that after his discussion of the prophetic and apocalyptic modes, Emmerson concludes that the first half of the poem is prophetic, but "ultimately the poet adopts the Christian apocalyptic view that salvation is not the result of a national or social renovation within time but is achieved by the individual through remaining faithful until the end when, after the oppression of Antichrist, the divine intervenes. The poem, therefore, analyzes the two related yet distinct outlooks on society, the church, and salvation that medieval Christians inherited from biblical literature, in the prophetic and the apocalyptic" (54). This is a fascinating view of the poem, but it is a view that, like other apocalyptic readings of the poem, fails to account sufficiently for Langland's continuing emphasis on the need for action, for doing well, better, and best, which surely require more than simply "remaining faithful until the end." This is not to deny that the poem contains apocalyptic elements. It is simply to say that the apocalyptic elements function within the context of Langland's prophetic stance. Thus, Langland certainly anticipated an apocalyptic event, perhaps even in the near future, but the anticipation of that event, especially in light of its presumed imminence, gave added urgency to his prophetic program. The closer he felt the apocalyptic moment to be, the more vital was the societal reform that he urged.

One possible reason for the critical emphasis on Langland's apocalypticism might be the fear of making him too Pelagian, too interested in the efficacy of works. Murtaugh, for example, points out the potential conflict between Langland's hopes for a society reformed in the image of God and "the Christian vision of the City of God which perfects the Earthly City only by supplanting it and by ending time" (31). This contradiction — that works are important, yet the world is not — may be inherent in the Christian view; but in his reliance on the biblical prophets Langland seems to ignore it, by accepting the world as the given sphere of action, and he defuses the charge of Pelagianism (if, indeed, he cared about such a charge). He is, after all, delivering a biblical message, adapted to the needs of his time; and he is emphatically not talking about an effort to hasten the advent of the end of time. He is simply describing how, in biblical terms, this world can be made a better place in both an individual and a communal sense, as it was in the early days of the Church, which he describes in the early history of Unity. Langland's intention in adopting his prophetic stance, in picturing himself, in all humility, as a mouthpiece for divine teaching, was to transform professed belief into real belief and then into action. Such a stance required a fairly literal understanding of biblical texts, that is, an emphasis on the literal rather than on the allegorical levels of the texts; but as Beryl Smalley and others have shown, such an understanding was available in the late Middle Ages. Langland's poem, too, is best understood on a literal level.

Let me conclude, then, by repeating something I said earlier: this study of *Piers Plowman* is not meant to displace other views of the poem. In fact I hope it can be used to support other readings of the poem as a whole and of its key scenes by providing a background against which they can be set. There is so much to find in *Piers Plowman* that no single reading of the poem can ever be enough. What we must remember is what Blenkinsopp says about Amos: "There is no going back on his basic message, that a society which neglects justice and righteousness does not deserve to survive" (96). Langland, like the prophets, wanted to help his society to survive.

Notes

Chapter I.

1. See Lawton 1981, 793.

Chapter II.

1. This discussion, incidentally, does not depend on the chronology of biblical redaction. Even if the Pentateuch achieved final form after Isaiah, the prophet clearly bases his teaching on well-known ideas.

2. Adolf Katzenellenbogen comments on the medieval view of this relationship: "In general, Jewish priesthood was considered to prefigure Christian priesthood. Yet the prophets also were regarded as prototypes .... During the struggle of investiture, writers saw in the prophets the prototypes of *sacerdotium*. Prophets had anointed kings and been their counselors. To Honorius Augustodunensis prophets and priests were almost the same. In secular affairs the prophets were subordinated to the kings while the kings were subjected to them in religious matters.... Hugh of Fleury ... believed that the priests in his own time held the power of the holy prophets" (33). This attitude may help to explain some of Langland's attitudes to the kings who appear in *Piers Plowman*.

3. Walter Ong reinforces Bloomfield's points when he explains that in the oral culture of the Middle Ages, when the Bible was read in public, when school consisted so much of listening to disputation about Scripture, "The air was filled with the word of God. It is evident enough from medieval literature generally that, although the percentage of persons who had formally studied the Scriptures or theology was always minuscule, the Bible was quite familiar to society at large" (268-69).

4. It is noteworthy that in Hebrew, though not in Latin, the root for the words translated as "eat" and "devour" are the same, which relates the verses even more closely.

5. It may be interesting for the reader to compare this treatment of the chapter with that in Alter (142-46).

6. And we might recall Boccaccio's statement in his "Short Treatise in Praise of Dante" that "theology is nothing other than a poetry of God" (Minnis 1988, 498).

7. G. R. Evans notes that according to Haymo of Auxerre, "Prophecy is characteristic of the Old Testament, not of the New; only the Apocalypse in the New Testament can be called prophetical in the strict sense of the term" (116).

8. For example, Jerome interprets the four creatures that bear the Divine Chariot as the Evangelists, and he adds that the human face represents all of Israel, the lion represents the ruling scepter of Judah, the calf represents the priestly and Levitical tribes, and the eagle represents God's vengeance, while the sets of wings that are joined from above represent heavenly prophecy (11-16). For Gregory, the combination of four faces on each creature represents faith, the four wings represent contemplation (which is insufficient without works, which are represented by the creatures' feet), and the four hands represent the four directions and the four virtues (33-37).

9. The literal meaning of the Hebrew word for prophet, *nabi,* seems to be a person who speaks on behalf of another, as Moses spoke for God. We can see the distinction in a passage from I Kings. When Saul and his servant decide to consult Samuel in search of their lost asses, the narrator inserts the following: "Now in time past, in Israel when a man went to consult God he spoke thus: Come, let us go to the seer [*ro'eh*]. For he that is now called a prophet [*nabi*], in time past was called a seer" (9:9). The word "prophet" does indeed come from the Greek for "speak before," but it means "to speak before" in a physical rather than in a temporal sense. That is, a prophet speaks before the people rather than before the things he talks about happen. The latter function, in the Hebrew, might more properly belong to the seer, which, in Hebrew as in English, derives from a root that means "to see."

10. As Torrell illustrates, the author of this treatise was indebted to other discussions of prophecy by Philip the Chancellor, William of Auxerre, Peter the Lombard, and others.

11. Passus I begins

What the montaigne bymeneth and þe merke dale
And the feld ful of folk y shal ȝou fair shewe.

12. See Salter 1983, 113, and Davlin's article on *Piers* and the Wisdom books.

13. As Kirk says, "Although the content of Piers's religion is not 'Old Testament,' the contractual psychology of it is" (1972, 77).

14. Peter says that "it may be shown that the teachings of both the Old and New Testaments are contained in this book" (Minnis 1988, 107).

15. Minnis points out that "Clerks who were at University to become qualified preachers sought in the human *auctores* of Scripture models which they could imitate. . . . The Scriptural *auctor* was being regarded in the role of preacher. . . ." (1984, 138). And Phyllis Roberts notes that "Master Langton in his preaching once compared the preacher to a messenger who announces the

mandates of the Lord to the people. He drew for his sources for themes, examples, and similitudes from the fountain of Scripture. The sermons, furthermore, draw abundantly on biblical texts by way of direct quotation. . . . Here too Langton has drawn widely on the books of the Old and New Testament. Most prominent are the prophetic books, major and minor" (99).

Chapter III.

1. An effective picture of the state of court affairs in 1372 is provided by Donald Howard: "It is now four years since the Duchess Blanche died: John of Gaunt is married to the young Princess Costanza . . . Katherine Swynford has that year borne the duke a son. . . . The French wars have begun again, and Gaunt is steadily abroad. The Black Prince is back in England, mortally ill. The king is in his dotage, Alice Perrers is forever about him, the court is gossiping shamelessly: There is cynicism in the air. . . ." (43).

2. According to Hudson, for Wyclif "The aim of the contemporary church should be the closest adherence to the teaching of Christ as set out in the gospels, and the imitation of the practice of the early church revealed in the Pauline and Petrine epistles and Acts . . ." (251).

3. David Jeffrey says, "To my knowledge Wyclif does not discuss the 'form' or intrinsic genre of the classical poets, nor does he deal in any of his printed volumes with the logic of their interpretation. He does deal with the form which should pertain to contemporary writing, in which, in his simplest version . . . 'the Christian should express himself under the authority of Scripture in the words of Scripture according to the form of Scripture.' That is, we can see that writing for the contemporary Christian would draw its sense of intrinsic genre from Scripture, and not from Vergil or Ovid" (134). Whether Langland knew Wyclif's thought or not, this is the path that he, too, followed.

4. Beryl Smalley tells us that in Wyclif's commentary on Isaiah, "Isaias' prophecy against the pride of Israel (Isa. xlvii.8) can apply to England; her pretensions will surely be abased in proportion to her guilt. To Baruch's question 'who shall enter into the treasure house of wisdom?' (iii.15), Wyclif answers that it will not be infidels or lords called nobles, such as were the idolatrous gentiles in the prophets' time" (1964, 267). And Janet Coleman, commenting on *Piers Plowman* B.III.93-100, says, "Langland next expresses a very common medieval attitude that current history is to be understood as having been prefigured in Scripture. Langland even confuses his texts, quoting in fact from Job when he intends to cite Solomon the wise king, in order to show that mayors and men who are responsible for maintaining law were warned that their homes should be devoured by fire if they accepted bribery. The events of 1381 are justified by the Old Testament, and this is seen as unfolding in recurring cyclical patterns" (1981a, 81).

5. It is interesting to note, in light of Wyclif's reliance on Scripture and Langland's practice of speaking biblically, Russell Peck's observation that John Ball "begins both his letters with a deliberately Pauline formula: 'John Ball, Saint Mary Priest, greeteth well all manner of men . . ." etc. (Cf., "Paul, apostle of Christ, greets God's beloved saints . . ." etc., with which Paul commonly begins his epistles.) (114).

6. Some critics, like Robertson and Huppé, see Will dressed as a sheep, a costume that they interpret *in malo*: "the dreamer is clothed as if he were a 'shepe'; that is, he resembles the false prophets in sheep's clothing of the Gospel (Matt.7.15)" (33). It is true that he wears different kinds of clothing, and that his clothing operates on a symbolic level, but in every other case he wears human clothing. More to the point is Holloway, who says that Dante, "in *Paradiso* XXV.7 speaks of his garb as a 'vello' [fleeceskin] and of returning in it from exile to his 'bello ovile' [fair sheepfold] of St. John's in Florence. Will, in the A and B Texts of *Piers Plowman*, is clad in a sheepskin, like a sheep" (4). She sees this as the garb of the pilgrim. I would argue that Will begins the poem dressed like a shepherd, following the example of Amos.

7. Murtaugh says that Langland "tends, almost in spite of himself, to glorify minstrels and lunatics and fools. In each revision, this was a cause of discomfort to him because he knew that most of these people in the real world were scoundrels and loafers. In the C/text, many of the references are cut or turned against the minstrels. But C introduces some new figures, the 'lunatik lollers' (C.X.107) who wander 'witlees' just as 'Peter dude and Paul' (C.X.111-112). They have the gift of prophecy. . . . In the end of the poem, the only men who stand by Conscience and go into the besieged barn of Unity are these same happy-go-lucky types. . . . The class in society which seems least amenable to law is the only one to rally to the defense of leute" (52).

8. Szittya asks why Langland so often links minstrels and friars. Part of the reason is Franciscan tradition, but another part is that "Langland uses minstrelsy as a metaphor for the use (or abuse) of the divine gift of speech, which enjoys an exalted conception in the poem. . . . Throughout the poem Langland maintains a distinction between professional minstrels and those who use their divine gift of speech properly. Only the latter, no matter what their profession, are true minstrels, 'goddes glemen,' while the professional entertainers are 'gedelynges,' abusing a divine gift shamelessly, sinfully, and in hope of getting gold" (253-54).

9. As Szittya says, "Insofar as the dreamer is a beggar, he is, like all other mendicants in the poem, potentially what Langland calls 'goddes minstrale.' I would maintain that 'goddes minstrale' is something far different and much better: a prophet" (267).

10. Bowers says that "When Will swoons for joy at hearing Piers' name (B.xvi.18-22) or has a dream 'as Crist wolde' (B.xiii.21-23), we feel that the dreams may well be sanctioned from above. But when the visions are described

with phrases like 'a ferly of Fairye' (B.prol.6) or 'as it sorcerie were, a sotil þyng wiþ alle' (B.xv.12), then there is cause for doubt. The cumulative effect is one of pervasive uncertainty about the trustworthiness of these dreams..." (29). As I hope to show, Will learns that his dreams are not untrustworthy. It is hard to imagine that the kinds of dreams Will has are the result of sloth.

11. For instance, in Ezekiel's first chapter the prophet uses comparison rather than direct statements: "He saw the semblance of four creatures; the soles of their feet resembled the sole of a calf's foot; in the midst of the creatures was an appearance like burning coals of fire resembling torches.... Such a mode of expression corresponds exactly to the manner in which we describe a dream" (Lindblom 125).

Chapter IV.

1. I am not arguing here that Will is Langland and that these lines are part of Langland's autobiography. The autobiography is as fictional as Will.

2. Anne Middleton makes the point that Langland would not have been proposing anything revolutionary here when she says that for Chaucer and his contemporaries, poetry was meant to be " 'a common voice' or to serve the 'common good' " (1978, 95).

3. Middleton says that in this passus, "Will is invited by Reason and Conscience, who seem about to charge him under the Statutes of Labor as an 'idle man,' to account for his stewardship. Somewhat surprisingly, he is released upon his resolution to begin to 'turn his time to profit.' [One wonders whether there might be a pun here.] But if the activity he intends is 'making,' its nature, subject, and place among other human crafts and estates are left maddeningly unclear, though some analogy between poetry and prophecy is several times suggested" (1978, 104).

4. According to Margaret Goldsmith, Piers' wife "bears a phrasal name with religious overtones: 'Werche-whanne-tyme-is' is fairly certainly an adaptation of half a text from *Gal.* 6:10. It would be entirely in Langland's manner to signal with half a text that half a truth was being ignored. A reader who recognizes the Pauline echo will be aware that the verse sums up a passage about 'doing well' [cp. *Gal.* 6:9] expressed in the metaphor of sowing and reaping. Since Paul is there contrasting 'sowing in the flesh' and 'sowing in the spirit', there is a covert reminder to clerical readers . . . of the vital difference between carnal and spiritual work" (39). So Paul provides another source for this name.

5. Clopper sees some confusion in the translation of the word "visio." According to Clopper, "The word *visio* suggests 'vision' or 'prophetic dream' to readers of the poem because *Piers Plowman* is a visionary poem. But the basic meaning of visio is 'sight' or 'act of seeing.' The *Visio* is the sight of those things in the world that are visible" (1985, 6). While Clopper's definition of the term

certainly is appropriate for *Piers Plowman*, he does not explain its use by so many of the prophets.

6. It is interesting to note that in the so-called Z-Text, we find the following lines near the poem's opening:

As y byheld in the est, an hey to the sonne,

Y sey a tour on a toft tryeliche ymaked,

A dep dale bynethe, as dym as a cloude:

Hit thondred, as me thouȝhte, there ant nawhere elles.

                                                              (I.14-17)

Someone, whether it was Langland or a copyist, included in this opening description the kind of meteorological activity that accompanied the revelation at Sinai and the initial revelation to Ezekiel.

7. Isaiah's injunctions are, of course, quite general and commonplace, but their import, "Cease to do perversely, learn to do well," corresponds to the import of Langland's words, and this correspondence is reinforced when we consider how much of *Piers Plowman* is devoted to exploring what "Learn to do well" means. The reference to Luke 6:40 in these lines — "The disciple is not above his master: but everyone shall be perfect, if he be as his master" — serves as a commentary on the earlier thought.

8. I do not claim, of course, that Isaiah is the sole source of this episode. As Yunck has shown, Lady Meed has a long, if not particularly distinguished lineage. But Langland's use of her here and the structure of these opening passus are inspired by the first chapter of Isaiah.

9. See, for example, I.63; IV.194; VI. 240-44; XII.52-55; XIV.39-42; 199-201; XVII.132-135; 156-58; 252-54; 297-322; XVIII.150; 162-75; XX.26; 96-113; 264-68; XXI.10; 44-49; 136-40; 422.

10. A more developed study of the role of the Jews in Middle English literature can be found in my article on the subject, listed in the bibliography.

11. The same is true of the Wisdom books and of Revelation, though of course the latter was strongly influenced by the prophets.

12. Alford argues that Langland "*began* with the quotations, and from them, using the standard aids of a medieval preacher, derived the substance of the poem" (1977, 82). I agree that this is possible, but I would add that Langland would have read this concordance method back into the Bible, and would have seen the authors of biblical texts using it, as Jerome does in his commentaries for instance.

13. The same point could be made about a poem like *The House of Fame*, which Jeffrey has shown also has a prophetic element in its background.

14. I know that humility is not a word that is often used to describe Will. Most critics find him less attractive. Lorraine Stock, for example, says that he "proves to be his usual obnoxious self, for he impatiently, arrogantly interrogates *Liberum Arbitrium* about the nature of the union between the corporal body and the will" (470). He may indeed sound this way, but if that impression arises out

of his commitment, his yearning to understand and to bring about reform, I am not willing to condemn him for it. Similarly Szittya says that in Passus X, "Dame Study seems to take Will for one of those who, like the friars, frequent rich men's feasts and raise sophistic questions about theology only to find contradictions in Scriptural or ecclesiastical teaching." But, Szittya points out, Study is wrong — Will may seem like that, but he is not.

15. These chapters are often called the "Isaiah Apocalypse," as the editors of the Oxford Annotated Bible explain, largely "because of their use of eschatological themes found in later apocalyptic writing."

16. As Barney points out, the whole episode contains an abundance of "ifs" (1973, 290).

17. In the *Exposicio textus Matthei xxiv*, Wyclif does a verse-by-verse commentary on Matthew 24, showing how each verse applies to the present, including wars, pestilence, and earthquakes (Szittya 177).

Chapter V.

1. As Szittya tells us, "The loosing of Satan had occurred and was occurring in history, Wyclif believed, though he was reluctant to identify it too precisely with a particular date or event. Since the truth of Scripture is eternal, Scriptural prophecy is often ambiguous and may be fulfilled in events of many different ages. . . . Wyclif concedes that Satan may have been unleashed to plague the world at various times in the first millennium after Christ, but he clearly feels the prophecy of Apoc. 20:7 is fulfilled more dramatically by events within the past two hundred years . . ." (163).

2. It is also worth noting that the last section of Ezekiel is a description of the restored Temple, which might have influenced Langland.

3. For a valuable discussion of Langland's views on social and individual salvation, see Robert Adams' article on "Langland's Theology" in *A Companion to Piers Plowman*, listed in the bibliography.

4. As Adams notes in dealing with the Pardon scene, "The heart of the priest's objection to the terms of Truth's pardon seems to be that it requires performance, whereas he would presumably prefer God's *mede* to be identical with earthly *mede* — defined by its complete disregard for any merit or demerit in recipient" (1983, 411). The priest is perfectly happy to proclaim his faith. He just does not want to have to do anything.

Bibliography

Editions of *Piers Plowman*

Piers Plowman: The A Version, revised edition. Ed. George Kane. Berkeley: University of California Press, 1988.
Piers Plowman: The B Version, revised edition. Ed. George Kane and E. Talbot Donaldson. Berkeley: University of California Press, 1988.
Piers Plowman by William Langland: An Edition of the C-Text. Ed. Derek Pearsall. Berkeley: University of California Press, 1978.
Piers Plowman: The Z Version. Ed. A. G. Rigg and Charlotte Brewer. Toronto: Pontifical Institute of Medieval Studies, 1983.

BIBLICAL

Unless otherwise noted, quotations from biblical texts are from *The Holy Bible*, the Douay Reims Version.

Wyclif Bible — Quotations are from *The Holy Bible, Containing the Old and New Testaments, with the Apocryphal Books, in the Earliest English Versions made from the Latin Vulgate by John Wycliffe, and his Followers* 4 vols. Ed. Sir Josiah Forshall and Sir Frederic Madden. Oxford: Oxford University Press, 1850. Reprinted, 1982.

MANUSCRIPTS

I have consulted the following manuscripts at the Walters Art Gallery in Baltimore, Maryland: MS.W.24, MS.W.30, MS.W.57, MS.W.59, and MS.W.79.

BOOKS AND ARTICLES

Adams, Robert. "Piers's Pardon and Langland's Semi-Pelagianism." *Traditio* 39 (1983): 366-418.

— — —. "The Reliability of the Rubrics in the B-Text of *Piers Plowman*." *Medium Aevum* 54 (1985): 208-31.

— — —. "Langland's Theology." In *A Companion to Piers Plowman*. Ed. John A. Alford. Berkeley: University of California Press, 1988.

Aers, David. *Chaucer, Langland and the Creative Imagination*. London: Routledge and Kegan Paul, 1980.

Alford, John. "The Role of the Quotations in *Piers Plowman*." *Speculum* 52 (1977): 80-99.

— — —. *Piers Plowman: A Glossary of Legal Diction*. Cambridge: D.S. Brewer, 1988.

— — —, ed. *A Companion to Piers Plowman*. Berkeley: University of California Press, 1988.

Alter, Robert. *The Art of Biblical Poetry*. New York: Basic Books, 1985.

Ames, Ruth. *The Fulfillment of the Scriptures: Abraham, Moses, and Piers*. Evanston, IL: Northwestern University Press, 1970.

Aquinas, St. Thomas. *Summa Theologiae*, vol. 45. Trans. and ed. Roland Potter O.P. New York: McGraw Hill, 1969.

Auerbach, Erich. *Mimesis: The Representation of Reality in Western Literature*. Trans. Willard Trask. Garden City: Anchor Books, 1957.

— — —. "Figura." In *Scenes from the Drama of European Literature*. Gloucester, MA: Peter Smith, 1973.

Augustine, St. *City of God*. Trans. Gerald Walsh, Demetrius Zema, Grace Monahan, Daniel Honan. Garden City: Image Books, 1958.

— — —. *De civitate Dei*. Ed. Bernardus Dombast and Alphonsus Kalb. CCLS, Vols. 47-48.

— — —. *De genesi ad litteram*. Ed. J.-P. Migne. Patrologia Latina, vol. 41. Paris, 1841.

— — —. *The Literal Meaning of Genesis*. Trans. John H. Taylor. New York: Newman Press, 1982.

Baldwin, Anna P. *The Theme of Government in Piers Plowman*. Cambridge: D.S. Brewer, 1981.

Barney, Stephen A. "The Plowshare of the Tongue: The Progress of a Symbol from the Bible to *Piers Plowman*." *Mediaeval Studies* 35 (1973): 261-93.

— — —. "Allegorical Visions." In *A Companion to Piers Plowman*, ed. John Alford. Berkeley: University of California Press, 1988.

Blenkinsopp, Joseph. *A History of Prophecy in Israel*. Philadelphia: Westminster Press, 1983.

Bloomfield, Morton W. "Joachim of Flora: A Critical Survey of his Canon, Teachings, Sources, Biography and Influence." *Traditio* 13 (1957): 249-311.

— — —. *Piers Plowman as a Fourteenth-century Apocalypse*. New Brunswick, NJ: Rutgers University Press, 1961.

Bogdanos, Theodore. *Pearl: Image of the Ineffable*. University Park, PA: The Pennsylvania State University Press, 1983.

Bowers, John M. *The Crisis of Will in Piers Plowman.* Washington, D.C.: Catholic University of America Press, 1986.

Cable, Thomas. "Middle English Meter and its Theoretical Implications." *Yearbook of Langland Studies* 2 (1988): 47-69.

Carruthers, Mary. *The Search for St. Truth.* Evanston, IL: Northwestern University Press, 1973.

— — —. "Time, Apocalypse, and the Plot of *Piers Plowman.*" In *Acts of Interpretation: The Text in its Contexts, 750-1600.* Ed. Mary J. Carruthers and Elizabeth D. Kirk. Norman, OK: Pilgrim Books, 1982.

Clopper, Lawrence M. "The Contemplative Matrix of *Piers Plowman* B." *Modern Language Quarterly* 46 (1985): 3-28

— — —. "Langland's Markings for the Structure of *Piers Plowman.*" *Modern Philology* 85 (1988): 245-55.

Coleman, Janet. *Piers Plowman and the Moderni.* Rome: Edizioni di Storia e Letteratura, 1981a.

— — —. *Medieval Readers and Writers, 1350-1400.* New York: Columbia University Press, 1981b.

Crowley, Robert, ed. *The Vision of Pierce Plowman, 1571?*

Daniel, E. Randolph, ed. *Liber de Concordia Novi et Veteris Testamenti. By Abbot Joachim of Fiore..* Philadelphia: American Philosophical Society, 1983.

Dante. *The Divine Comedy.* Ed. and trans. Charles S. Singleton. Princeton: Princeton University Press, 1975.

Davlin, Mary Clemente, O.P. *Piers Plowman and the Books of Wisdom. Yearbook of Langland Studies* 2 (1988): 23-33.

Deuchler, Florence, Jeffrey Hoffeld, and Helmut Nickel, eds. *The Cloister Apocalypse.* New York: Metropolitan Museum of Art, 1971.

Donaldson, E. Talbot. *Piers Plowman: The C Text and Its Poet.* New Haven: Yale University Press, 1949.

Donna, Rose Bernard. *Despair and Hope: A Study in Langland and Augustine.* Washington, DC: Catholic University of America Press, 1948.

Emmerson, Richard K. "The Prophetic, the Apocalyptic, and the Study of Medieval Literature." In *Poetic Prophecy in Western Literature.* Ed. Jan Wojcik and Raymond-Jean Frontain. Cranbury, NJ: Associated University Presses, 1984.

Evans, G. R. *The Language and Logic of the Bible: The Earlier Middle Ages.* Cambridge: Cambridge University Press, 1984.

Forrester, Duncan. "Biblical Interpretation and Cultural Relativism." In *Ways of Reading the Bible.* Ed. Michael Wadsworth. Totowa, N.J.: Barnes and Noble, 1981.

Fowler, David C. *The Bible in Middle English Literature.* Seattle, WA: University of Washington Press, 1984.

Frank, Robert W., Jr. *Piers Plowman and the Scheme of Salvation: An Interpretation of Dowel, Dobet, and Dobest.* New Haven: Yale University Press, 1957.

Friedman, Richard E. "The Prophet and the Historian: The Acquisition of Historical Information from Literary Sources." In *The Poet and the Historian.* Ed. Richard E. Friedman. Chico, CA: Scholars Press, 1983.

Geller, Stephen. "Were the Prophets Poets?" *Prooftexts* 3 (1983): 211-21.

Goldsmith, Margaret E. *The Figure of Piers Plowman: The Image on the Coin.* Cambridge: D.S. Brewer, 1981.

Gower, John. *The Major Latin Works of John Gower.* Trans. Eric W. Stockton. Seattle, WA: University of Washington Press, 1962.

Gregory, St. *Homiliae in Hiezechihelem prophetam.* Ed. Marcus Adriaen. CCLS, vol. 142.

Guttman, Julius. *Philosophies of Judaism.* Trans. David W. Silverman. New York: Schocken Books, 1973.

Hailperin, Herman. *Rashi and the Christian Scholars.* Pittsburgh: University of Pittsburgh Press, 1963.

Hargreaves, Henry. "The Wycliffite Versions." In *The Cambridge History of the Bible,* vol. 2. Ed. G. W. H. Lampe. Cambridge: Cambridge University Press, 1969.

Hillers, Delbert. *Covenant: The History of a Biblical Idea.* Baltimore: Johns Hopkins University Press, 1969.

Holloway, Julia Bolton. *The Pilgrim and the Book.* New York: P. Lang, 1987.

Howard, Donald R. *Chaucer: His Life, His Works, His World.* New York: E.P. Dutton, 1987.

Hudson, Anne. "Wycliffite Prose." In *Middle English Prose.* Ed. A. S. G. Edwards. New Brunswick, NJ: Rutgers University Press, 1984.

Jeffrey, David Lyle. "Chaucer and Wyclif: Biblical Hermeneutic and Literary Theory in the XIVth Century." In *Chaucer and Scriptural Tradition.* Ed. David Lyle Jeffrey. Ottawa: University of Ottawa Press, 1984.

— — —. "Sacred and Secular Scripture: Authority and Interpretation in *The House of Fame.*" In *Chaucer and Scriptural Tradition.* Ed. David Lyle Jeffrey. Ottawa: University of Ottawa Press, 1984.

Jerome, St. *Commentariorum in Hiezechielem.* Ed. Francisci Florie. CCLS, vol. 75.

— — —. *Commentarium in Esaiam.* Ed. Marcus Adriaen. CCLE, vols. 73, 73A.

John of Salisbury. *Frivolities of Courtiers and Footprints of Philosophers. Being a Translation of the First, Second, and Third Books and Selections from the Seventh and Eighth Books of the Policraticus of John of Salisbury.* Trans. Joseph B. Pike. Reprint of 1938 ed. New York: Octagon Books, 1972.

Justice, Steven. "The Genres of *Piers Plowman.*" *Viator* 19 (1988): 291-306.

Kane, George. "Langland and Chaucer: An Obligatory Conjunction." In *New Perspectives in Chaucer Criticism.* Ed. Donald M. Rose. Norman, OK: Pilgrim Books, 1981.

Kaske, R. E. "Patristic Exegesis in the Criticism of Medieval Literature: The Defense." In *Critical Interpretations of Medieval Literature: Selected Papers from the English Institute, 1958-1959.* Ed. Dorothy Bethurum. New York: Columbia University Press, 1960.

Katzenellenbogen, Adolf. *The Sculptural Programs of Chartres Cathedral.* New York: W.W. Norton, 1959.

Kaufmann, Yehezkel. *The Religion of Israel.* Trans. and abr. Moshe Greenberg. New York: Schocken Books, 1972.

Kaulbach, Ernest N. "The 'Vis Imaginativa Secundum Avicennam' and the Naturally Prophetic Powers of *Ymaginatif* in the B-Text of *Piers Plowman.*" *Journal of English and Germanic Philology* 86 (1987): 496-512.

Kirk, Elizabeth D. *The Dream Thought of Piers Plowman.* New Haven: Yale University Press, 1972.

– – –. "Langland's Plowman and the Recreation of Fourteenth-Century Religious Metaphor." *Yearbook of Langland Studies* 2 (1988): 1-21.

Kugel, James L. *The Idea of Biblical Poetry: Parallelism and Its History.* New Haven: Yale University Press, 1981.

Lampe, G. W. H. "The Exposition and Exegesis of Scripture to Gregory the Great." In *The Cambridge History of the Bible*, vol. 2. Ed. G. W. H. Lampe. Cambridge: Cambridge University Press, 1969.

Lawton, David A. "Lollardy and the *'Piers Plowman'* Tradition." *Modern Language Review* 76 (1981): 780-93.

– – –. "Middle English Allterative Poetry: An Introduction." In *Middle English Alliterative Poetry and Its Literary Background.* Ed. David Lawton. Cambridge: D.S. Brewer, 1982.

– – –. "The Unity of Middle English Alliterative Poetry." *Speculum* 58 (1983): 72-94.

Leclercq, Dom Jean. "The Exposition and Exegesis of Scripture from Gregory the Great to St. Bernard." In *The Cambridge History of the Bible*, vol. 2. Ed. G. W. H. Lampe. Cambridge: Cambridge University Press, 1969.

Leff, Gordon. *Heresy in the Middle Ages: The Relation of Heterodoxy to Dissent, c.1250-c.1450.* New York: Manchester University Press, 1967.

Lewis, C. S. *A Preface to Paradise Lost.* London: Oxford University Press, 1961.

Lindblom, J. *Prophecy in Ancient Israel.* Philadelphia: Fortress Press, 1962.

McFarlane, K. B. *John Wycliffe and the Beginnings of English Nonconformity.* London: English Universities Press, 1952.

Macrobius. *Commentary on the Dream of Scipio.* Trans. William Harris Stahl. New York: Columbia University Press, 1952.

Martin, Priscilla. *Piers Plowman: The Field and the Tower.* London: Macmillan Press, Ltd., 1979.

Mattuck, Israel. *The Thought of the Prophets.* London: Allen & Unwin, 1953.

Middleton, Anne. "The Idea of Public Poetry in the Reign of Richard II." *Speculum* 53 (1978): 94-119.

— — —. "The Audience and Public of *Piers Plowman*." In *Middle English Alliterative Poetry and Its Literary Background*. Ed. David Lawton. Cambridge: D.S. Brewer, 1982a.

— — —. "Narration and the Invention of Experience: Episodic Form in *Piers Plowman*." In *The Wisdom of Poetry*. Ed. Larry D. Benson and Siegfried Wenzel. Kalamazoo: Medieval Institute Publications, 1982b.

— — —. "Introduction: The Critical Heritage." In *A Companion to Piers Plowman*. Ed. John A. Alford. Berkeley: University of California Press, 1988.

Mills, David. "The Role of the Dreamer in *Piers Plowman*." In *Piers Plowman: Critical Approaches*. Ed. S. S. Hussey. London: Methuen & Co. Ltd., 1969.

Minnis, Alastair J. "Chaucer and Comparative Literary Theory." In *New Perspectives in Chaucer Criticism*. Ed. Donald M. Rose. Norman, OK: Pilgrim Books, 1981.

— — —. *Medieval Theory of Authorship: Scholastic Literary Attitudes in the Later Middle Ages*. London: Scolar Press, 1984.

— — — and A. B. Scott, eds. *Medieval Literary Theory and Criticism, c.1100-c.1375*. Oxford: Clarendon Press, 1988.

Morse, Ruth, ed. *St. Erkenwald*. Cambridge: D.S. Brewer, 1975.

Murtaugh, Daniel M. *Piers Plowman and the Image of God*. Gainesville, FL: University Presses of Florida, 1978.

Nicholson, E.W. *Preaching to the Exiles: A Study of the Prose Tradition in the Book of Jeremiah*. New York: Schocken Books, 1971.

Nolan, Barbara. *The Gothic Visionary Perspective*. Princeton: Princeton University Press, 1977.

Norton-Smith. John. *William Langland*. Leiden: E.S. Brill, 1983.

Olan, Levi A. *Prophetic Faith and the Secular Age*. New York: Ktav Publishing House, 1982.

Ong, Walter J. *The Presence of the Word: Some Prolegomena for Cultural and Religious History*. New Haven: Yale University Press, 1967.

Owst, G.R. *Literature and Pulpit in Medieval England*, 2nd ed. New York: Barnes and Noble, 1961.

Packe, Michael. *King Edward III*. Ed. L. C. B. Seaman. London: Routledge and Kegan Paul, 1983.

Pantin, W.A. *The English Church in the Fourteenth Century*. South Bend, IN: University of Notre Dame Press, 1962.

Parlement of the Thre Ages. Ed. M. Y. Offord. Early English Text Society, Original Series, No. 246. Oxford University Press, 1959.

Pearsall, Derek. *Old English and Middle English Poetry*. London: Routledge and Kegan Paul, 1977.

— — —. *Piers Plowman by William Langland: An Edition of the C-Text*. Berkeley: University of California Press, 1978.

Peck, Russell A. "Social Conscience and the Poets." In *Social Unrest in the Late Middle Ages*. Ed. Francis X. Newman. Binghamton: Medieval and Renaissance Texts and Studies, 1986.

Pierce the Ploughman's Crede. Ed. Walter W. Skeat. Early English Text Society, Original Series, No. 30. London: N. Trubner & Co., 1867.

Reeves, Marjorie. *The Influence of Prophecy in the Later Middle Ages: A Study in Joachimism*. Oxford: Oxford University Press, 1969.

Robbins, Rossell Hope. "Dissent in Middle English Literature: The Spirit of (Thirteen) Seventy-six." *Medievalia et Humanistica* 9 (1979): 25-51.

Robert of Basevorn. *The Form of Preaching*. In *Three Medieval Rhetorical Arts*. Ed. James J. Murphy. Berkeley: University of California Press.

Roberts, Phyllis Barzillay. *Studies in the Sermons of Stephen Langton*. Toronto: Pontifical Institute of Medieval Studies, 1968.

Robertson, D.W., Jr. and Bernard Huppé. *Piers Plowman and Scriptural Tradition*. Princeton: Princeton University Press, 1951.

St. Jacques, Raymond. "The Liturgical Associations of Langland's Samaritan." *Traditio* 25 (1969): 217-30.

Salter, Elizabeth. *Piers Plowman: An Introduction*. Oxford: Blackwell, 1969.

— — —. *Fourteenth-Century English Poetry: Contexts and Readings*. Oxford: Clarendon Press, 1983.

Sapegno, Natalino. "How the *Commedia* Was Born." In *From Time to Eternity: Essays on Dante's Divine Comedy*. New Haven: Yale University Press, 1967.

Shepherd, Geoffrey. "English Versions of the Scriptures before Wyclif." In *The Cambridge History of the Bible*. Ed. G. W. H. Lampe. Cambridge: Cambridge University Press, 1969.

Sidney, Sir Philip. "An Apologie for Poetrie." In *Elizabethan Critical Essays*. Ed. G. Gregory Smith. Oxford: Oxford University Press, 1904.

Smalley, Beryl. "A Commentary on Isaias by Guerric of Saint-Quentin, O.P." *Studi e testi* 122 (1946): 383-97.

— — —. *The Study of the Bible in the Middle Ages*. Notre Dame: University of Notre Dame Press, 1964.

— — —. "Wyclif's *Postilla* on the Old Testament and his *Principium*." In *Oxford Studies Presented to Daniel Callus*. Oxford: Clarendon Press, 1964.

— — —. "The Bible in the Medieval Schools." In *The Cambridge History of the Bible*. Ed. G. W. H. Lampe. Cambridge: Cambridge University Press, 1969.

— — —. *The Gospels in the Schools, c.1100-c.1280*. London: The Hambledon Press, 1985.

Spearing, A.C. *Medieval Dream-Poetry*. Cambridge: Cambridge University Press, 1976.

Stacey, John. *John Wyclif and Reform*. Philadelphia: Westminster Press, 1964.

Steinberg, Theodore L. "The Jewish Presence in Middle English Literature." *Christian-Jewish Relations* 20 (1987): 29-48.

Steinmann, Jean. *Saint Jerome*. Trans. Ronald Matthews. London: Geoffrey Chapman, 1959.

Sterne, Laurence. *The Life and Opinions of Tristram Shandy, Gentleman*. Ed. James A. Work. New York: Odyssey Press, 1940.

Stock, Lorraine. "Will, Actyf, Pacience, and *Liberum Arbitrium*: Two Recurring Quotations in Langland's Revisions of *Piers Plowman C-Text*, Passus V, XV, XVI." *Texas Studies in Language and Literature* 30 (1988): 461-77.

Szittya, Penn R. *The Antifraternal Tradition in Medieval Literature*. Princeton: Princeton University Press, 1986.

Torrell, Jean-Pierre. *Theorie de la prophetie et philosophe de la connaissance aux environs de 1230: La contribution d'Hughes de Saint-Cher*. Louvain: Spicilegium sacrum Lovaniense, 1977.

Traver, Hope. "The Four Daughters of God: A Mirror of Changing Doctrine." *Publications of the Modern Language Association* 40 (1925): 44-92.

Trower, Katherine B. "Temporal Tensions in the *Visio* of *Piers Plowman*." *Medieval Studies* 35 (1973): 389-412.

Turville-Petre, Thorlac. *The Alliterative Revival*. Ipswich, England: D.S. Brewer, 1977.

Vasta, Edward. *The Spiritual Basis of Piers Plowman*. The Hague: Mouton, 1965.

Von Nolcken, Christina. "*Piers Plowman*, the Wycliffites, and *Pierce the Plowman's Creed*." *Yearbook of Langland Studies* 2 (1988): 71-102.

Ward, James M. *Hosea: A Theological Commentary*. New York: Harper & Row, 1968.

Wells, Henry W. "The Construction of *Piers Plowman*. *Publications of the Modern Language Association* 45 (1929): 123-40.

Yunck, John A. *The Lineage of Lady Meed: The Development of Medieval Venality Satire*. South Bend, IN: Notre Dame University Press, 1963.